Holly George-Warren

GRATEFUL DEAD 365

ABRAMS, NEW YORK

"They're not the best at what they do—they're the only ones that do what they do." Legendary concert promoter Bill Graham devised that slogan for signage welcoming the Dead and their fans to the band's last show at Winterland in San Francisco. The sentiment would be expressed time and again, as at this Cal Expo concert (at left) photographed by Susana Millman. The Dead's shows—dating back to 1965 and their days as the Warlocks (when they were captured by Paul Ryan's camera)—would beckon Deadheads for three decades. The Dead and their audience have retained a close-knit, reciprocal relationship like no other in the history of rock. Nearly forty years after Woodstock, and more than a dozen since Jerry Garcia's passing, the Grateful Dead's legacy remains more potent than that of any other American band since the birth of rock & roll.

Here, then, is a photographic tribute to and celebration of the Grateful Dead. This book is dedicated to the Deadheads of the world—past and present—who turned a rock & roll band into a lifestyle. It would be foolhardy to attempt a complete document of the band—in words or photographs—so instead, think of *Grateful Dead 365* as a flashback of sorts, a series of images representing the many facets and phases of the band's life, and beyond (all the way to February 2008). Hopefully, some of the images will be new ones for even the most ardent of Deadheads; other shots are those iconic ones beloved by all. Photographers who got up close and personal with the band, including Baron Wolman, Jim Marshall, Herb Greene, Peter Simon, Jay Blakesberg, and Susana Millman, add an intimacy to the proceedings. Such rock photographers as Robert Altman, Amalie R. Rothschild, Stephanie Chernikowski, Ebet Roberts, and Bob Leafe also captured some special Dead moments. And the inimitable Stanley Mouse has provided samples of the extraordinary artwork he created for the Dead.

Tracking the band's circuitous journey is not easy, but it sure is fun! (As for any potholes I hit along the way, please let me know about them.) Enjoy the trip.

—Holly George-Warren

Introduction

The Warlocks at the In Room, 1965 photograph by Paul Ryan/Getty Images

001

It all started with the Warlocks. To be more exact, Jerry Garcia, Bob Weir, and Pigpen had originally played together in the acoustic Mother McCree's Uptown Jug Champions. And Bill Kreutzmann had played with Garcia and Pigpen in the R&B-style party band the Zodiacs. But it was the electric garage combo the Warlocks that morphed into the Grateful Dead. Bassist Phil Lesh, guitarist Bob Weir, drummer Bill Kreutzmann, guitarist Jerry Garcia, and, on keyboards, harmonica, and percussion, Pigpen (from left) began gigging around the Bay Area in early '65. They honed their still somewhat limited chops with a six-week residency at the appropriately named In Room, a bar in Belmont. Playing five sets of covers, the Warlocks took on early rock & roll, R&B, blues, hillbilly, and folk—everything but jazz (the music of their greatest influence, John Coltrane). Garcia, born on August 1, 1942, in San Francisco, had been playing in numerous bluegrass and folk outfits, including a duo with his then wife, Sara.

Pigpen, 1965 photograph by Paul Ryan/Getty Images

002

Born on September 8, 1945, in San Bruno, California, Ron McKernan became "Pigpen" thanks to his personal hygiene habits. According to Dead biographer Dennis McNally, "He had a motorcycle chain permanently bolted to his wrist and wore oily jeans, Brando-esque T-shirts, and greasy hair." The charismatic Pigpen lived and breathed the blues: He played harp, tambourine, and percussion; could handle all kinds of blues and R&B vocals; and noodled on a Vox Continental organ, which he later traded for a more soulful Hammond B-3. In the early Warlock (and Dead) days, he shared the front-man spot with Jerry Garcia. The two music obsessives originally crossed paths in their hometown of Palo Alto in 1961—the first of the future Dead to meet.

Bill Kreutzmann, 1965 photograph by Paul Ryan/Getty Images

003

Like Garcia and Pigpen, Bill Kreutzmann hailed from Palo Alto, where he was born on May 7, 1946. Kreutzmann, who had been playing drums since childhood, was married, worked in a wig shop, and taught drumming on the side. When he joined the Warlocks, he was considered Palo Alto's best drummer. "The only drummer I had really played with around that area that I thought really had a nice feel was Bill," Garcia later said.

Bob Weir, 1965

004

The youngest member of the Warlocks was Bob Weir, born on October 16, 1947 (bassist Phil Lesh was the oldest, born on March 15, 1940, in Berkeley). As a teenager, Weir wandered into a Palo Alto music store where Garcia gave guitar and banjo lessons (and Kreutzmann taught drumming). Before long, Weir was playing washtub bass and jug in a combo with Garcia. The two were recruited by Pigpen to play electric guitar in the Warlocks, with seventeen-year-old Weir holding down rhythm while Garcia played lead.

The Grateful Dead, c.1966 photograph by Hulton Archive/Getty Images

005

By the end of 1965, the band had changed its name to the Grateful Dead, after Phil Lesh discovered a 45 rpm single by another ensemble called the Warlocks. The group briefly used the name the Emergency Crew to record a demo for Autumn Records. On November 12 of that year the band gathered around a copy of *Funk & Wagnalls New Practical Standard Dictionary*, which Garcia randomly opened to a page, blindly pointing his finger. "There was *grateful dead*, big black letters edged all around in gold, man, blasting out at me, such a stunning combination [of words]!" he later recalled. Here, Kreutzmann, Weir, Pigpen, Garcia, and Lesh (from left) pose for an early portrait.

Family Dog poster, 1966 poster by Wes Wilson

006

The Family Dog was a venture originally created by four San Francisco housemates (including artist Alton Kelley) who organized a dance at the Longshoremen's Hall on October 16, 1965. While the Jefferson Airplane and the Charlatans played, the tripped-out audience grooved to Bill Ham's light show. Two more such psychedelic get-togethers followed. In 1966, Texan Chet Helms took over the name and put on Family Dog dances at the Avalon Ballroom, located at Sutter and Van Ness. Helms managed Big Brother, with Janis Joplin, and bills at the Avalon frequently featured them, plus the Airplane, Quicksilver Messenger Service, and the Grateful Dead. Exceptional artists created intriguing posters for the shows, with Kelley, Victor Moscoso, Wes Wilson, Stanley Mouse, and Rick Griffin leading the pack.

THE QUICK and THE DEAD

GRATEFUL DEAD

QUICKSILVER MESSENGER SERVICE

JUNE 10-11

PLUS→ THE NEW TWEEDY BROTHERS

AVALON • • • BALLROOM

ON SUTTER AT VAN NESS IN SAN FRANCISCO AT 9 P.M.

"Don't look for premiums or coupons as the cost of the tobacco blended in CAMEL cigarettes prohibits the use of them." TICKET OUTLETS: San Francisco—Discount Records, 262 Sutter; Bally Shoes; Music 5, 5th & Market; City Lights Book Store; Psychedelic Shop; Cedar Alley Coffee House. Oakland—Cal Records, 1320 Broadway; Stairway. Berkeley—Cal Records, 2350 Telegraph; Record City, 234 Telegraph. San Mateo—Record Specialist, Hillsdale Mall. San Carlos—Kramer's, 765 Laurel.

Family Dog poster, 1966 poster by Victor Moscoso

007

Family Dog poster artists were interested in nineteenth-century graphics and advertising motifs—as seen through the "experienced" eyes of the scene surrounding the Merry Pranksters' Acid Tests. Their endeavors gave birth to the psychedelic style that would symbolize the Summer of Love the following year. This poster by Victor Moscoso featured a rather diabolical St. Nick in honor of the yuletide performances featuring the Dead, the Steve Miller Blues Band, and Moby Grape.

Family Dog poster, 1966 poster by Stanley Mouse and Alton Kelley

008

Stanley Mouse (b. Miller), an artist from Detroit who started his career airbrushing hot-rod art, landed in San Francisco the first night of the Trips Festival, in 1966. He fell in with the Family Dog scene and met poster artists Wes Wilson and Victor Moscoso, who introduced him to Chet Helms. Mouse became friendly with Maine native and art-school dropout Alton Kelley and began creating Family Dog posters, sometimes collaborating with Kelley, who specialized in lettering and collage. The most iconic emblem of the Dead, the skull and roses motif, was first developed as a Family Dog poster by Mouse and Kelley. This pen-and-ink creation, promoting a September 16–17 show, was based on a nineteenth-century illustration by E. J. Sullivan featured in *The Rubaiyat of Omar Khayyam*. Collectively and individually, Mouse and Kelley would also create several Dead album covers over the years. According to Paul Grushkin's definitive study of the genre *The Art of Rock*, more San Francisco poster art was devoted to the Grateful Dead than to any other band.

GRATEFUL DEAD

OXFORD CIRCLE

AVALON BALLROOM

SUTTER at VAN NESS S.F.

FAMILY DOG PRESENTS

Family Dog poster, 1967 <small>poster by Rick Griffin</small>

Before moving to San Francisco in 1966, Los Angeleno Rick Griffin, another art-school dropout, created the Murph the Surf character and other eye-catching SoCal graphics, often published in *Surf* magazine. After meeting Mouse and Kelley, he became part of the Big Five of Family Dog poster artists. "Mustachioed aliens, potbellied surf rats, crazed Disney characters, top-hatted Indians, Trojan warriors, tiki gods, cowboys, skulls, cobras, beetles, fetuses, hordes of wriggling sperm, armies of anthropomorphized eyeballs, fearsome horned creatures of various sorts, a praying mantis in work boots playing a violin and . . . Jesus—the cast reads like some crazy eruption of the collective American subconscious," said the *Los Angeles Times* about Griffin's work. Many of the aforementioned characters would grace Grateful Dead posters and album covers.

TICKET OUTLETS -
SAN FRANCISCO: MNASIDKA (HAIGHT-ASHBURY), CITYLIGHTS BOOKS (NO. BEACH), KELLY GALLERIES (3681-A SACRAMENTO), THE TOWN SQUIRE (1318
POLK ST), BALLY LO SHOES (UNION SQ), HUT T-1 STATE COLLEGE, BERKELEY: MOES BOOKS, DISCOUNT RECORDS, SAUSALITO: TIDES BOOKSTORE,
REDWOOD CITY: REDWOOD HOUSE OF MUSIC (720 WINSLOW). SAN MATEO: TOWN & COUNTRY MUSIC CENTER (4TH & EL CAMINO), LA MER CAMERAS &
MUSIC (HILLSDALE BLVD AT 19TH). MENLO PARK: KEPLER'S BOOKS & MAGAZINES (825 EL CAMINO). SAN JOSE: DISCORAMA (235 S. FIRST ST)

(c) FAMILY DOG PRODUCTIONS 639 GOUGH ST, San Francisco, Calif 94102

RICK GRIFFIN —

The Grateful Dead at the Fillmore Auditorium, c. 1966

photograph by Michael Ochs Archives/Getty Images

010

In San Francisco, the Dead constantly played concerts at the Fillmore Auditorium. Bill Graham, who booked the Fillmore, frequently paired the Dead with the Jefferson Airplane. On December 31, 1966, the Dead played the first of twenty New Year's Eve shows for Graham, a tradition that would continue nearly every year up until 1991. The Dead would gig at the Fillmore throughout 1966 and the first half of 1967, with an array of acts on the bill, including the Doors, Chuck Berry, Love, and the Paul Butterfield Blues Band. Onstage this night are Pigpen on organ, Garcia, Lesh, Kreutzmann, and Weir (from left).

Phil Lesh and Bob Weir at Monterey Pop, 1967

011

On Sunday, June 18, 1967, the Grateful Dead played the final evening of the legendary, three-day Monterey Pop Festival. They later dismissed their Sunday performance as being subpar—they played between incendiary sets by the Who and Jimi Hendrix (Otis Redding and Big Brother, featuring Janis Joplin, also played some of their best gigs ever). Dubious of the commerciality of the event and their lackluster showing, the Dead did not allow their set, which opened with "Viola Lee Blues," to be part of an ensuing film of the event. The song had been featured on the band's self-titled debut album, released by Warner Bros. in March of that year.

Pigpen and Veronica Grant, 1967 photograph by Jim Marshall

012

The year 1967 ushered in the Summer of Love, with its epicenter San Francisco and its birth marked by the Human Be-In in Golden Gate Park on January 14. Free concerts abounded, and the Grateful Dead took part in many. Here, Pigpen makes the scene with his paramour Veronica Grant.

Jerry Garcia, 1967 photograph by Jim Marshall

013

Jerry Garcia had earned the nickname Captain Trips as a participant in Ken Kesey's Acid Tests. With the Grateful Dead, he became ringleader of the Summer of Love's favorite party band. Photographer Jim Marshall, who chronicled the scene's top groups—including the Dead, the Jefferson Airplane, the Charlatans, and Big Brother (with Janis Joplin)—believes this shot was taken at a free concert in Golden Gate Park, probably in April of that year.

Bob Weir at the Hollywood Bowl, 1967 photograph by Michael Ochs Archives/Getty Images

014

On Friday, September 15, 1967, the Grateful Dead played the Hollywood Bowl with the Jefferson Airplane and Big Brother. The concert was entitled Bill Graham Presents the San Francisco Scene in Los Angeles. The eighteen-thousand-seat venue was the largest for the band to date, but Weir seems perfectly relaxed while waiting for the rehearsal to get under way.

Jerry Garcia at the Hollywood Bowl, 1967 photograph by Michael Ochs Archives/Getty Images

015

With his Gibson SG Les Paul–model guitar, Garcia appears ready for action during rehearsal. Two weeks earlier, the band had played a tiny club in Rio Nido, California, and performed for the first time "Dark Star," the song by Robert Hunter and Jerry Garcia that would inspire future jam bands the world over.

Bill Kreutzmann at the Hollywood Bowl, 1967 photograph by Michael Ochs Archives/Getty Images

016 Bill Kreutzmann looks lonely while waiting for rehearsal to start. But soon enough, he would have a partner on drums; he had just met Mickey Hart in San Francisco, and not long after there would be two drum kits holding down the Dead's back line.

Bob Weir at the Hollywood Bowl, 1967 photograph by Michael Ochs Archives/Getty Images

017

Bobby Weir was a month shy of his twentieth birthday when this shot was taken at the Hollywood Bowl concert rehearsal. According to the band's road manager Jonathan Reister, "Bobby was our little juvenile delinquent." Garcia, apparently, was dismayed at his failure to progress on electric guitar—he played more like an acoustic picker than a rhythm guitarist. "Most of the band fights were about his guitar playing," Reister later said.

Drug bust, 1967 photograph by Baron Wolman

018

On October 2, 1967, the San Francisco Police Department's narcotics squad raided the Grateful Dead's home at 710 Ashbury Street. They turned up approximately a pound of pot and hash. Pigpen and Bob Weir, both of whom had forsworn drugs, were arrested, along with managers Danny Rifkin and Rock Scully, crew member Bob Matthews, and various friends, including Veronica Grant, Sue Swanson, and Toni Kaufman (daughter of Beat poet Bob Kaufman). Here, Rifkin, Grant, Matthews, Swanson, Pigpen, Kaufman, and Weir (from left) get released on bail.

The Dead at home, 1967 photograph by Baron Wolman/Retna

019

The Grateful Dead held a press conference on October 5, 1967, and photographer
Baron Wolman was among those attending. His photographs and coverage of the
bust would be featured in the first-ever issue of a new music paper, *Rolling Stone*,
which hit the streets on November 9. Here, after the press conference, the Dead
pose as outlaws on their front stoop: Bill Kreutzmann, Rock Scully, Jerry Garcia,
Pigpen, Bob Weir, Phil Lesh, and Danny Rifkin (clockwise from left).

Press conference, 1967 photograph by Baron Wolman/Retna

020

With hippies being denounced by newsman Harry Reasoner on a TV special, the San Francisco police were out to make scapegoats of the Grateful Dead. Ironically, in their raid of the Dead's "way-out 13 room pad," as it was described by the *San Francisco Chronicle*, they missed a kilo of pot hidden in a cupboard. The band enlisted pal Harry Shearer (of future *This Is Spinal Tap* and *The Simpsons* fame) to write their statement to the press. Over coffee with whipped cream and cookies, spokesperson Danny Rifkin told the press, "Almost anyone who has ever studied marijuana seriously and objectively has agreed that, physically and psychologically, marijuana is the least harmful chemical used for pleasure and life enhancement." Months later, the drug charges would result in those arrested paying small fines. Seen here, Pigpen, Kreutzmann, Lesh, Scully, Rifkin, Weir, Garcia, and attorney Michael Stepanian (from left).

The Grateful Dead at San Quentin, 1968 photograph by Dister/Dalle/Retna

021

On Thursday, March 7, 1968, the Dead performed a free concert on a flatbed truck outside San Quentin State Prison (Johnny Cash would record his famous live album inside the prison the following year). Four days earlier, the band had played a free concert on a flatbed truck in the Haight. It was a kind of farewell to their home since 1966—increasing police presence and an onslaught of tourists and teenage runaways had done away with the neighborhood's laid-back charm. Soon, the Dead would disperse to various homes, primarily in Marin County.

Dancing Dead fan, 1968 photograph by Baron Wolman

022

Baron Wolman recalled a festive gig that the Dead played at San Francisco's waterfront: "It was really relaxed and fun—the waterfront wasn't built up at all then." Wolman was particularly taken with this ecstatic Dead fan and shot several frames of her Isadora Duncan–style dance—perhaps the original version of what would later be called the "Woodstock sun grope."

Pigpen and Jerry Garcia, c. 1968 photograph by Jim Marshall

023

"Jerry Garcia was one of the most accessible of all the artists I've shot," asserts Jim Marshall. "I knew Jerry almost from day one with the Grateful Dead, and there were never any conditions about taking his picture." Pigpen seems cooperative in this shot, though some photographers would find him less willing to face the camera.

Mickey Hart, 1968 photograph by Michael Ochs Archives/Getty Images

024

In September 1967, at a Dead concert at San Francisco's Straight Theater, Mickey Hart joined in on "Alligator," at Bill Kreutzmann's behest. And as Dead biographer Dennis McNally puts it, "They finished the song, and the band included six people." Hart was born Michael Steven Hartman in Brooklyn, New York, in 1943. His father was a musician but had deserted the family when Hart was just a toddler; Hart began playing drums at age ten. He eventually rejoined his father, Lenny, who ran a drum store in San Francisco. Hart and Kreutzmann met at a Count Basie show at the Fillmore; the "Alligator" episode occurred only a month later.

Weir, Hart, Garcia, and Lesh, 1968 photograph by Michael Ochs Archives/Getty Images

025

The Grateful Dead had plenty to celebrate in the summer of '68: The single "Dark Star" was released in May, and their second album, the experimental *Anthem of the Sun* ("a complete mindblower," according to the *NME*), was issued in July. The band played numerous well-received shows in New York. After a concert in Central Park on May 5, *The Village Voice* raved, "No tricks, just music, hard, lyric, joyous— pure and together, dense and warm as a dark country summer night. There's the Dead and then there's everybody else."

The Grateful Dead at the bus stop, 1968 photograph by Michael Ochs Archives/Getty Images

026

In San Francisco, the Dead frolic in the street near their Potrero Hill studio. Music journalist Michael Lydon wrote of them, "Certainly they are the weirdest—black satanic weird and white archangel weird. As weird as anything you can imagine, like some horror comic monster who, besides being green and slimy, happens also to have seven different heads, a 190 IQ, countless decibels of liquid fire noise communication, and is coming right down to where you are to gobble you up."

The Dead at the Newport Pop Festival, 1968 photograph by Jim Marshall

027

On August 4, 1968, the Grateful Dead were among the bands to perform at the first Newport Pop Festival, held in Costa Mesa, California. Mel Lawrence, who helped with the festival's production, recalls that the stage was perched on the parking lot of the Orange County Fairgrounds—not the most idyllic of spots. Featured artists included the Animals, the Byrds, Canned Heat, Iron Butterfly, Electric Flag, Quicksilver Messenger Service, and the Jefferson Airplane—the latter of whom engaged in a cream-pie fight with the Dead, Lawrence remembers. Pictured here are Pigpen on his Hammond B-3, Jerry Garcia, and Phil Lesh (from left).

The Dead hang out, 1968 photograph by Michael Ochs Archives/Getty Images

028

Where was Pigpen on this day of revelry? Perhaps he was curled up with a bottle of hooch, a bunch of blues records stacked on the turntable, and a female friend. Later in the year, both he and Weir would be fired for not performing up to snuff— but the dismissal didn't stick.

Mickey Hart, 1968

029

The Grateful Dead had been enjoying LSD since they first participated in the Merry Pranksters' Acid Tests in late 1965. Hart began tripping soon after he moved to San Francisco, and apparently was so inspired by one psychedelic experience that he created decorative drumheads for his father's drum shop. According to fellow drummer Kreutzmann, acid "wasn't a drug, it was an endless roller-coaster ride."

Pigpen and Rock Scully at Sky River Festival, 1968 photograph by Jim Marshall

030

The Grateful Dead played the Sky River Festival on Monday, September 2, 1968.
This rural event was held at Betty Nelson's Organic Raspberry Farm, near Sultan,
Washington. The band arrived after playing an afternoon benefit concert, followed
by a Fillmore gig the evening before. Things at Sky River ended with a bang when
band members joined blues legends Big Mama Thornton and James Cotton onstage.

Load-out, 1968 photograph by Michael Ochs Archives/Getty Images

031

The Grateful Dead became famous for the massive amounts of sound equipment that accompanied them on the road. In the early days, though, travel cases were a bit simpler. Here, Kreutzmann and Lesh lug, while Garcia, Hart, and Weir collapse behind.

Jerry Garcia at the Fillmore West, 1968 photograph by Jim Marshall

032

The effects of the Fillmore's light show give a trippy feel to this double-exposed portrait of Jerry Garcia. Bill Ham and Glenn McKay pioneered the innovative psychedelic light shows at San Francisco theaters. In July '68, Bill Graham closed his original Fillmore Auditorium and opened the Fillmore West in an old ballroom that had previously been the Carousel Ballroom, a joint venture of the Dead and the Jefferson Airplane. The Grateful Dead played a four-night run at the Fillmore West November 7–10.

Pigpen at the Fillmore West, 1968 photograph by Jim Marshall

033

Beginning in August 1967, Pigpen took over lead vocals on a number that would become a showcase for his raspy instrument: "Turn On Your Love Light." The song brought down the house when the charismatic bluesman turned the Bobby Bland hit into a lengthy vamp. In June 1969, Janis Joplin would join Pig on the number at a Fillmore West gig. Pigpen got the red-light treatment when performing "Love Light" at the Fillmore, possibly in November '68.

Golden Gate Park, 1969 photograph by Robert Altman/Retna

034

On Wednesday, May 7, 1969, the Grateful Dead played a huge outdoor concert at the Polo Field at San Francisco's Golden Gate Park, scene of the first Be-In in 1967. Grace Slick, vocalist of the Jefferson Airplane, who shared the bill, once commented, "From an audience standpoint . . . the Airplane was more accessible. . . . The Grateful Dead looked like they were almost dead. . . . They were a *bizarre*-looking group of people." Here, Jerry Garcia surveys the crowd.

Aoxomoxoa liner shot, 1969 photograph by Michael Ochs Archive/Getty Images

035

With Pigpen front and center, seen here are Dead members and friends, including a young Courtney Love, whose father hung out with and briefly worked for the band. Warner Bros. promoted the June release of the album with a Pigpen look-alike contest, advertised in various teen mags. Its name a palindrome, *Aoxomoxoa* was the Dead's first self-produced effort, and all eight tracks featured lyrics by Robert Hunter. Garcia later told Dead chronicler Blair Jackson, "A lot of the *Aoxomoxoa* songs are overwritten and cumbersome to perform. But at the time, I wasn't writing songs for the band to play—I was writing songs to be writing songs."

The Grateful Dead with Tom "TC" Constanten, 1969

photograph by Herb Greene/Michael Ochs Archives/Getty Images

036

In November 1968, an erudite keyboardist who Phil Lesh had known at Berkeley in '61 joined the band. At the time, Weir and Pigpen had been given their walking papers—though they didn't. In any case, Tom Constanten took over keys, while Pig was relegated to congas. Constanten can be heard on *Aoxomoxoa* and *Live/Dead,* which documented several '69 shows and was released in November of that year. Constanten, who never really gelled with Hart or Weir, left the band in 1970. Herb Greene, who began shooting the band in '65, took this publicity shot for Warner Bros.—Constanten, Weir, Kreutzmann, Garcia, Pigpen, Hart, and Lesh (from left).

Jerry Garcia, 1969 photograph by Baron Wolman/Retna

037

Rolling Stone chief photographer Baron Wolman photographed the Dead in May 1969 for the August 23 issue. In a variation on this pose, Garcia became cover boy for *RS* #40, with the cover line GOOD OLE GRATEFUL DEAD running under the sole other headline, THE DOPE CRISIS. Garcia had a love-hate relationship with the zine and the press in general; the band frequently felt it'd been misquoted in interviews and thus didn't sit down with journalists very often. Jerry's amputated finger is proudly displayed in his salute here, but was hidden on *Rolling Stone*'s cover. He would grace its cover seven more times, four by himself, once with the band, and twice posthumously.

Bob Weir, 1969 photograph by Baron Wolman/Retna

038

"Weir occupied an often underappreciated yet truly fulcrumatic role in the Dead," according to the official bible of Dead arcana *Grateful Dead: The Illustrated Trip*. "The man that the women in the audience most noticed—standing between two instrumental geniuses [Garcia and Lesh]—he was at times dismissed as a rocker who could only rev up a Chuck Berry tune and close a show. Not true. . . . Weir gave the Dead a necessary creative alternative. If Garcia had been the only singer and songwriter, it would not have been the Grateful Dead."

Pigpen, 1969 photograph by Baron Wolman/Retna

039

With TC in the band, Pigpen no longer got to attack the keyboards. But as a vocalist, he continued to squall the blues like no one else in the band, as well as play a righteous harmonica. "No matter how screwed up on LSD and how crazy it got for us," contended former manager Rock Scully, "you could always look to Pigpen to bring you down to earth and be there for you. Even musically, when the band was going way, way out in 'Dark Star,' they knew they could listen to Pig and have some sense of where they were. . . . When Garcia's guitar turned into a snake, Pigpen saw it as a guitar, and Jerry could rely on him to do that."

Mickey Hart, 1969 photograph by Baron Wolman/Retna

040

While Pigpen and Weir served their "probation," the other Dead members formed
Mickey and the Hartbeats to perform the kind of improvisational jams they felt
the pair couldn't handle. Hart, Lesh, Garcia, and Kreutzmann played six shows
as Mickey and the Hartbeats between October and December 1969. Guest
musicians such as Elvin Bishop and Jack Casady would sit in. Weir remembered
of this brief period, "Jerry and Phil in particular thought we were sort of holding
things back. The music wasn't able to get as free because it was hog-tied by our
playing abilities—which was kind of true."

Bill Kreutzmann, 1969 photograph by Baron Wolman

041

In this portrait, Baron Wolman captured Bill Kreutzmann the buckaroo. In fact, several members of the Dead besides Kreutzmann enjoyed horseback riding, usually indulging in the activity at Mickey Hart's ranch in Novato, California. The Marin County spread was also the scene of target shooting. The cosmic-cowboy look had been around since the Charlatans, and in Los Angeles the Flying Burrito Brothers had taken to wearing rhinestoned Nudie suits.

Tom "TC" Constanten, 1969 photograph by Baron Wolman

042

Born in 1944, avant-gardist TC Constanten grew up in Las Vegas. A student of astrophysics at Berkeley, Constanten would study with such noted experimentalists as composers Karlheinz Stockhausen and Luciano Berio. In the mid-1960s, Constanten joined the air force before the draft could get him. While in the service, he contributed a tape of electronic music and edgy keyboards to be edited into "That's It for the Other One" on *Anthem of the Sun*. Upon his military discharge in November 1968, he joined the Dead.

Phil Lesh, 1969 photograph by Baron Wolman

043

Baron Wolman recalls that Phil Lesh was sick the day he photographed each member of the Grateful Dead in his San Francisco studio. So, once Lesh recovered, Wolman took his cameras to the bassist's Marin County home and snapped him there. Here, with his six-shooter stuck in his belt, Lesh relaxes amid the flora and fauna.

The Fillmore East, 1969 photograph by Amalie R. Rothschild

044

In March 1968, Bill Graham opened the Fillmore East in New York's East Village, on the corner of Second Avenue and Sixth Street. A former Yiddish theater, then a converted movie palace, the venue became *the* place to see bands. Amalie R. Rothschild, then an NYU film-school grad student, began hanging out at the Fillmore soon after it opened. By the next year, Nikon in hand, she had turned into what one theater staffer called the venue's "candid camera." The Grateful Dead, who put on some of their best shows ever at the Fillmore, became one of her favorite subjects.

The Grateful Dead at the Fillmore East, 1969 photograph by Amalie R. Rothschild

045

"For a few short, memorable years, the Fillmore East is where we played it best," Mickey Hart wrote in his foreword to Rothschild's *Live at the Fillmore East*, documenting her photography at the theater. On this night, Jerry Garcia, Phil Lesh, and Bob Weir (from left) are bathed in a red glow. Among the theater's innovative lighting crew was Candace Brightman, who would eventually go on to work for the Dead, bringing her technical mastery to their tours.

Jerry Garcia onstage at the Fillmore East, 1969 photograph by Amalie R. Rothschild

046

Bill Graham once said the Fillmore East reminded him of a Bronx movie theater he'd gone to every Saturday afternoon as a kid. And in time, the Fillmore came to symbolize Bill Graham. "That area, the Lower East Side, was kind of a terrific place to have the Fillmore," Atlantic Records cofounder Ahmet Ertegun once reminisced. "There were elements of danger in going there. There were the motorcycle guys who would come wandering around whenever the Grateful Dead played. But nothing fazed Bill Graham." In fact, the Hells Angels almost stormed the place one night, demanding free entrance to a Dead show, but Graham wouldn't back down, even after being hit in the face with a tow chain. "I just stood there, wiped the blood off with my hand, and stared right back at them without saying a word," Graham recalled. "They just left. From that point on, there were really no problems with the Angels in New York."

Bill Graham watches the Dead, 1969 photograph by Amalie R. Rothschild

049

Though the Fillmore East staff preferred the Dead to any other band, according to Rothschild, they still had to watch their backs—mostly their beverages!—when the band played. Dosing drinks with LSD was commonplace among the Dead and their entourage. "It was a cardinal rule never to drink out of an open can or cup when the Dead were playing," says Rothschild, "unless we wanted to risk an unexpected acid trip." On this particular night, Bill Graham himself (far right, with drumstick and cowbell) had been dosed—and it wasn't the first time. As for Weir (at left, partially obscured) and Pigpen (center), by '69 the former had given up acid, and the latter always preferred booze to psychedelics.

Graham and Garcia backstage at the Fillmore East, 1969 photograph by Amalie R. Rothschild

Backstage at the Fillmore, Bill Graham seems to be enjoying the trip, as does Jerry Garcia. Graham first met Garcia at the Trips Festival in January 1966. Tripping heavily and mistakenly thinking his guitar was broken, Garcia was deeply touched when Graham tried to repair it. "Here's this guy who doesn't know anything about guitars," Garcia later recalled to Graham biographer Robert Greenfield, "and he's trying to fix mine. It was a sweet display. It was incredible. Always loved him for that. No matter how much he screams or what kind of tantrums he throws or anything. With me, he's never been able to shake that first impression of, 'Here is this helpful stranger.'"

The Dead onstage at the Fillmore East, 1969 photograph by Jay Good

051

TC and the Dead decided to part ways by the end of 1969. The avant-garde keyboardist had become a Scientologist, and the band did not appreciate his proselytizing. He'd also started a music-theater project called Tarot that he found more artistically satisfying than the Dead. "I wanted to be a bigger fish in a small pond," he later told Garcia biographer Blair Jackson, "and Tarot was more edifying." He'd play his last gig with the Dead in January 1970. Here, at the Fillmore East, are TC, Kreutzmann (partially obscured), Pigpen, Garcia, Hart (partially obscured), Lesh, and Weir (from left).

Jerry Garcia, c. 1969 photograph by Jim Marshall

052

"I think basically the Grateful Dead is not for cranking out rock & roll, it's not for going out and doing concerts . . . I think it's to get high. . . . To get really high is to forget yourself. And to forget yourself is to see everything else."

—Jerry Garcia

Bill Kreutzmann, 1970 painting by Stanley Mouse

053

To record their third studio album, the Dead turned to a new batch of noticeably country-flavored songs that Garcia had started writing. *Workingman's Dead* "seemed like a burnished artifact from the past, a lost treasure from the rich vein of music making that Folkways archivist Harry Smith mined for his *Anthology of American Folk Music*," noted Steve Silberman in his notes to the expanded reissue of the album, released by Rhino in 2001. "Even the sepia-toned cover . . . seemed to have been channeled from that homespun continuum." Mouse Studios produced that cover, and Stanley Mouse created a series of portraits for the back. Here, Mouse's watercolor version of his portrait of Bill Kreutzmann.

Bobby Weir, 1970 painting by Stanley Mouse

054

To create portraits for the back cover of *Workingman's Dead*, Mouse first photo-graphed each band member to use as a reference for the freehand airbrush artwork that would follow. Thanks to Mouse's long friendship with the band, each portrait has a natural, casual quality. He had lived catty-corner across the street from the Dead's 710 Ashbury headquarters, and Mouse Studios created the cover for the band's debut album in 1967.

Jerry Garcia, 1970 painting by Stanley Mouse

055

"Through the years, in between life's dramas, I caught glimpses of beauty, light, and form. These insights stuck to my inner being like secrets in the universe. Life's rambling often covered these wondrous undercurrents, but once in a while they would surface."

—Stanley Mouse

Phil Lesh, 1970 painting by Stanley Mouse

056

"When I think of Stanley Mouse, I think of his open-eyed fascination with the world around him, and if I were to pick a half dozen of the definitive 1960s people, Stanley would be one of them. If the earth were parting in front of Stanley, he'd probably say, *'Heeeeey, look at that!'* I think of Stanley as a smiling blotter, picking up everything."

—Bill Graham

Mickey Hart, 1970 painting by Stanley Mouse

057

"We're not in the entertainment business—we're in the transportation business.
We move minds."

—Mickey Hart

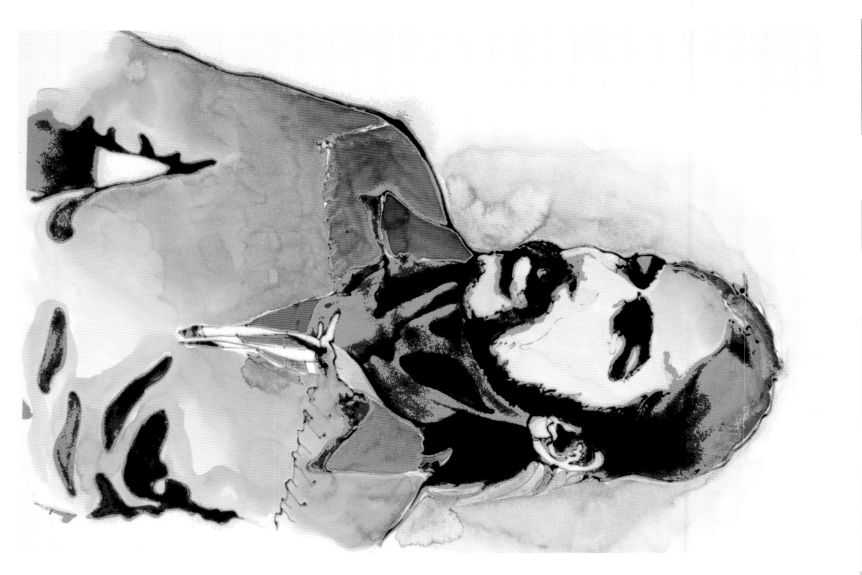

Pigpen, 1970 painting by Stanley Mouse

058

"He was the guy who really sold the band, not me or Weir. . . . Pigpen is what made the band work."

—Jerry Garcia

The Grateful Dead, 1970 photograph by Michael Ochs Archives/Getty Images

During a fall tour of northeastern colleges, the Dead became the subject of a Queens College newspaper editorial: "Are the Grateful Dead devils or angels . . . [with the] ability to drive people to peculiar heights of ecstatic frenzy . . . their whole beings absorbed, taken over." Here, Mickey Hart, Phil Lesh, Bob Weir, Bill Kreutzmann, Pigpen, and Jerry Garcia (from left).

The Dead onstage at the Fillmore East, 1970 photograph by Amalie R. Rothschild

060

The band kicked off the new decade with a spectacular show at the Fillmore East on January 2, 1970. "I consider this my definitive Fillmore East concert shot," says Rothschild, who, over a three-year period, took nearly twenty thousand photographs of such artists as the Who, Janis Joplin, Jimi Hendrix, and Van Morrison. "It was rare that I could get all the members of a band clearly visible with uniform lighting—and even rarer to be able to include and see the audience as well. It is fitting, using flash fill, that I was able to achieve this for a Dead picture, since they were practically the house band and our favorite."

Sold-out Dead show at the Fillmore East, 1970 photograph by Amalie R. Rothschild

061

Hordes of Grateful Dead fans milled around the outside of the Fillmore East trying to get into this sold-out show. By the summer, with the release of the critically and commercially successful *Workingman's Dead*, the band's fame would spread outside its core fan bases of California and New York. On January 2, 1970, the Fillmore East was "packed to the gills," Rothschild remembers. "I used flash fill to get the balcony and orchestra illuminated."

Live at the Family Dog, 1970 photograph by Robert Altman/Retna

062

On Wednesday, February 4, 1970, the Grateful Dead performed a concert for Chet Helms's Family Dog Productions at a venue called the Great Highway (which would be shuttered that summer). The psychedelic Avalon Ballroom, which had hosted such memorable Dead shows, promoted by Family Dog since 1966, had closed down in '68. "The best thing about it was that the audience all danced," Garcia once commented about the band's Family Dog gigs. "We were not performers. We were playing for our family, in a sense. It kind of had that feel, that informality." Here, Pigpen, Garcia, Kreutzmann, Lesh, and Weir (from left).

Ticket line at the Fillmore East, 1970 photograph by Amalie R. Rothschild

063

When it was announced in January 1970 that the Dead would be playing six shows (two performances nightly) over three evenings in February, fans flocked to buy tickets. Also on the bill: the Los Angeles psychedelic group Love, led by the magnetic Arthur Lee; and the Macon, Georgia, group that would come to define southern rock. The Allman Brothers, featuring brothers Duane and Gregg Allman, Dickey Betts, Jai Johanny Johanson, Butch Trucks, and Berry Oakley, were fairly unknown at the time; they had opened for Blood, Sweat & Tears at the Fillmore in December 1969. Though Love had had two hits, "My Little Red Book" (1966) and "7 and 7 Is" ('67), the Dead was clearly the draw.

Ticket line at the Fillmore East, 1970 photograph by Amalie R. Rothschild

064

After the Allman Brothers debuted at the Fillmore East, the staff wanted them back immediately. The Grateful Dead seemed the perfect bill for the jam-loving Georgia boys who also had two drummers. Staffer Allan Arkush recalled the impression the Allmans had made in December 1969: "They played four forty-five minute sets that [debut] weekend, and we couldn't get enough of them. We thought they were fabulous. The crew all voted to have the Allmans back." The fans who stood in line for tickets for one of these legendary February 11, 13, and 14 shows paid $5.50 for a mezzanine seat.

Ticket line at the Fillmore East, 1970 photograph by Amalie R. Rothschild

065

The revelry and camaraderie illustrated by this Rothschild shot presaged the Deadhead community that was on the horizon. Over the next decade, more and more folks would travel the country following the Grateful Dead.

Jam at the Fillmore East, 1970 photograph by Amalie R. Rothschild

066

Longtime Deadheads and aficionados cite the Grateful Dead's February 11, 13, and 14 shows in 1970 among the best of the band's three-decade career. On the first night, during the 11:30 set, Duane and Gregg Allman, Berry Oakley, and Butch Trucks joined the Dead onstage. Also sitting in were guitarist Peter Green and drummer Mick Fleetwood, whose group Fleetwood Mac had played with the Dead in New Orleans two weeks earlier (following one show, members of the Dead were arrested for drug possession). Fleetwood (far left, with arms outreached) later recalled dropping acid at the Fillmore: "I gooned around on the stage. . . . That was one of the crazed nights there." Rothschild's photographs are the only visual documents known to exist of this historic event.

Pigpen and the Allmans, 1970 photograph by Amalie R. Rothschild

067

During the February 11, 1970, Fillmore jam, Pigpen took the mic to sing his signature "Turn On Your Love Light" following the supergroup's improvisational takes on "Dark Star" and "Spanish Jam." Those who can remember say Pigpen's performance that night featured some of his "most inspired rapping." Rothschild recalls, "The late show, which started at 11:30, was amazing and the atmosphere was electric. The Allmans did a wonderful set and then the Dead came on close to 1:30. They played for about an hour and a half and at some point, I can't remember how it came about, members of the Allman Brothers Band joined in. It was a fabulous and historical moment and the vibes and the music were so terrific that I shot a few pictures. In 1997, I discovered that my photographs were the only visual record of that extraordinary jam when John Dwork, publisher of a Dead fanzine *Dupree's Diamond News,* tracked me down and first published one of them." Captured by Rothschild's camera are Pig, Garcia (obscured), Gregg Allman, Duane Allman, and Berry Oakley (clockwise from left).

Pigpen on percussion and Gregg Allman on organ, 1970

photograph by Amalie R. Rothschild

068

Pigpen must have been in heaven to be jamming with musicians nearly as steeped in the blues as he was. Some of the sets from those February gigs were surreptitiously tape-recorded, with the results passing hands among fans and becoming coveted possessions—a harbinger of a Deadhead tradition. "I have a cassette somewhere of Duane Allman, Peter Green, and Jerry Garcia jamming together," the Fillmore's Allan Arkush told journalist Robert Greenfield. "They played 'Dark Star' and the Donovan song 'There Is a Mountain'—which the Allmans turned into 'Mountain Jam' because of that night."

Backstage at the Fillmore East, 1970 photograph by Amalie R. Rothschild

069

Pigpen, Garcia, and Weir, accompanied by road manager Jon McIntyre (center, back)—soon to be promoted to manager—prepare for what would be a legendary set on February 11, 1970. Rothschild recalls getting the evil eye from Pigpen, and thus grabbing only one frame before leaving the Dead to themselves. "I was never certain what reception I would get when I decided to photograph scenes backstage," Rothschild reports. "But I did get the sense that Pigpen was staring me out and not wanting me to keep shooting—probably because I was using flash. It was quite dark backstage and impossible to photograph without flash, even though I normally shot black-and-white film rated at 800 ASA. I was always somewhat shy and didn't want to be seen as intruding on anyone's privacy, so it was a delicate situation when I shot backstage, and if anyone indicated they weren't happy about it I always stopped."

Owsley "Bear" Stanley backstage at the Fillmore East, 1970

photograph by Amalie R. Rothschild

070

In 1966, the great LSD chemist Owsley Stanley began working as the Grateful Dead's soundman. Nicknamed Bear, he constantly struggled to overcome the technical difficulties inherent in live shows. More as a means of documenting the Dead's sound quality than of capturing their performances, he began taping the group's sets every time he operated the PA. Fortunately, he was on duty during the three-night run at the Fillmore East (it was a rare occasion at the Fillmore when a soundman arrived with a band). He selected several acoustic numbers from the shows on February 13 and 14 for *History of the Grateful Dead, Vol. 1 (Bear's Choice)*. "I was interested in the tapes as a record of my work, like a diary," Bear wrote in the 1973 release's liner notes. Here, in a very rare shot (he did not like being photographed), Stanley prepares to create one of his "sonic journals" on February 11.

Jerry Garcia backstage at the Fillmore, 1970 photograph by Amalie R. Rothschild

073

Always up for a new challenge, Jerry Garcia honed his skills on pedal steel guitar. In March, as sideman to his friend David Crosby's group Crosby, Stills, Nash & Young, he played the distinctive pedal steel parts on "Teach Your Children," a massive hit from CSNY's chart-topping album *Déjà Vu*. During the summer of '69, Garcia had started a side project as steel guitarist with some old compadres in the group New Riders of the Purple Sage. (The 1912 novel *Riders of the Purple Sage,* by Zane Grey, was a major source for early Western movies, and the handle was also adopted by a Los Angeles–based singing cowboy combo in the 1940s.) When Rothschild took this photo of Garcia backstage at the Fillmore, on May 15, 1970, the Dead and NRPS were in the midst of their first tour together.

New Riders of the Purple Sage at the Fillmore East, 1970

photograph by Amalie R. Rothschild

074

As part of a concert series called An Evening with the Grateful Dead, the New Riders would kick off the show. Here making their debut at the Fillmore East on May 15, 1970, are: Mickey Hart on drums, John "Marmaduke" Dawson on acoustic guitar, David Nelson on electric guitar, Dave Torbert on bass, and Jerry Garcia on pedal steel (from left). "That first tour was fabulous," Dawson later said. "We had a built-in friendly crowd waiting for us—'Wow, what's this new thing that Garcia's up to?'" Columbia soon signed NRPS and released its self-titled album, featuring the same lineup, with Garcia also adding banjo. Phil Lesh, who played bass with the group early on, was the LP's executive producer.

Acoustic set at the Fillmore East, 1970 photograph by Amalie R. Rothschild

075

In addition to the NRPS opener, An Evening with the Grateful Dead also comprised an acoustic set by the Dead, along with one or two electric sets. At this May 15, 1970, show, Cold Blood, Buddy Miles, and the Guess Who were also on the Fillmore's bill. The catchy "Casey Jones" and acoustic "Uncle John's Band," from the forthcoming *Workingman's Dead*, were already getting FM airplay. The latter would be the first Dead single to chart on *Billboard*, reaching number 69 (its flip side was "New Speedway Boogie"). For "Uncle John's Band" to get airplay, however, the word *goddamn* had to be edited out of the radio version.

The electric Dead at the Fillmore East, 1970 photograph by Amalie R. Rothschild

076

With Dead fans and Fillmore staff packing the wings and backstage, the band goes electric at the Fillmore East. Later in the year, *Cashbox* would report that the Dead's "impact on the Fillmore audience was absolutely phenomenal, and their popularity continues to grow with every performance." Captured here are Garcia, Weir (on lead vocals), Kreutzmann, Lesh, Hart, and—playing a Hammond B-3 and sporting a Fillmore East jersey—Pigpen (from left).

The Grateful Dead, c. 1970 photograph by Chris Walter/Getty Images

077

Changes were brewing for the Dead. Mickey Hart would leave the group in
February 1971 to recover psychologically from a year's worth of trauma. His
father, Lenny Hart, had been managing the band, and it was discovered in early
'70 that he'd embezzled some $150,000. Lenny fled the country to avoid arrest;
his treachery nearly bankrupted the Dead, and his betrayal devastated his son.
Though the band held Mickey blameless, he needed a break from the stress and
constant touring and retreated to his Novato ranch. He wouldn't return to the
Dead for four years. On top of that, Pigpen began missing gigs because of ill
health. After collapsing not long after an August 1971 gig, he was hospitalized,
nearly dead from severely damaged internal organs, including his liver. He couldn't
play for three months, but after giving up hooch, he eventually returned to the
stage. Seen here, still together, Jerry Garcia, Bob Weir, Phil Lesh, Bill Kreutzmann,
Pigpen, and Mickey Hart (clockwise from left).

Paul Kantner, Grace Slick, Jerry Garcia, and Bill Graham, 1970

photograph by Larry Hulst/Getty Images

078

When this photo was taken in October 1970, recent tragic events had cast a pall over things: On September 18, Jimi Hendrix had died in London (the Dead found out at the Fillmore East), and two weeks later, on October 4, Janis Joplin had OD'd on heroin in Los Angeles. On the fourth and fifth, the Dead played at Bill Graham's Winterland with Slick and Kantner in the Jefferson Airplane, on a bill that also included sets by Quicksilver Messenger Service, NRPS, and Hot Tuna. Upon Janis's death, Garcia told *Rolling Stone*, "When she went out after something, she went out after it really hard, harder than most people ever think to do, ever conceive of doing. . . . She did what she had to do and closed her books. I don't know whether it's the thing to do, but it's what she had to do." Former paramour Pigpen reminisced, "We used to get drunk and play pool together. She beat me 80 percent of the time."

New Year's Eve at Winterland, 1970/71 photograph by Robert Altman/Retna

079

Over the course of 1970, the Dead played 120 gigs—their busiest year yet. (Former manager Rock Scully put the number at 145—maybe it just *felt* like that many.) In addition, they recorded the masterful Americana sequel to *Workingman's Dead*. *American Beauty*, released in November, featured the band's theme song of sorts, "Truckin'," which documented life on the road, making reference to their New Orleans pot bust. "What a long, strange trip it's been," the track's hook, became the slogan not just for the band, but for a generation. At their New Year's Eve Winterland show, balloons dropped from the ceiling at midnight, each conveying a tab of "orange sunshine." Yup, what a long, strange trip . . .

The Grateful Dead at the Fillmore East, 1971 photograph by Amalie R. Rothschild

080

Presaging the streamlined Dead, this set at the Fillmore East featured a quintet: Garcia, Kreutzmann, Lesh, Weir, and Hart (from left). Rock Scully described a typical night at the Fillmore in his memoir, *Living with the Dead*: "Long jams are the very air the Dead breathe. They can do half of *Anthem of the Sun*, "St. Stephen," "China Cat," and then it's like, 'Holy shit! We just got started— what time is it?' We get outside and it's daylight. We walk up to the Gem Spa at 6 a.m., buy a newspaper, and go have breakfast at Ratner's."

Jerry Garcia on pedal steel, 1971 photograph by Amalie R. Rothschild

081

New Riders of the Purple Sage and the Dead played a five-night run at the Fillmore East from April 25 to 29, 1971. Rothschild captured Garcia at close range, on April 27, onstage with NRPS. By that time, Garcia had contributed pedal steel to numerous recordings, including Paul Kantner's solo album *Blows Against the Empire*. "He went in and just experimented with sounds," Kantner later told Blair Jackson, "seeing what kind of sounds he could get out of it, running it through various pedals and echoes and delays. . . . Before that, he'd pretty much just been doing country licks on the steel, and this gave him the opportunity to get a little weirder, which he always appreciated."

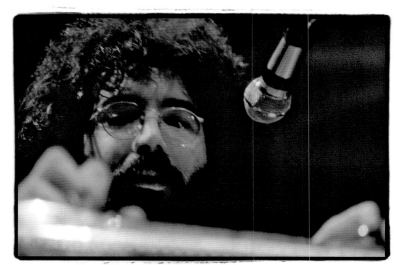
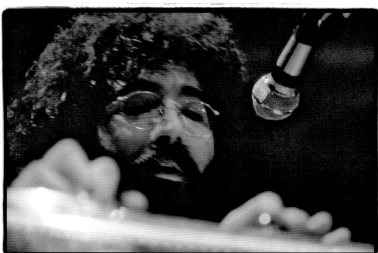
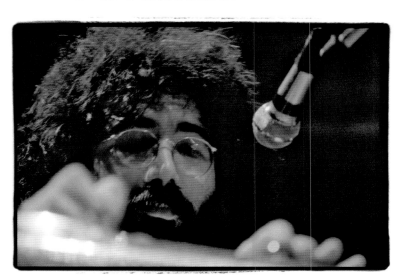

New Riders of the Purple Sage, 1971 photograph by Amalie R. Rothschild

082

David Nelson, Dave Torbert, and John "Marmaduke" Dawson (from left) harmonized on the band's country-rock songs, written by Dawson. Onstage at the Fillmore East on April 27, 1971, they wowed the crowds who packed the place five nights straight. "I guess we represented something to East Coast people that was missing from their lives," Dawson later theorized. "Maybe some of it was our disregard for the harsh realities of day-to-day life, which are always right in your face in the East, especially in New York City."

Last run at the Fillmore East, 1971 photograph by Amalie R. Rothschild

083

"[The] Fillmore East is like a piece of the true ark," Joshua White once commented. The Dead's five-night stand in April 1971 would constitute the band's final run at the legendary venue. The Fillmore closed its doors after its June 27 all-night show, featuring the J. Geils Band, the Allman Brothers, the Beach Boys, Albert King, and Mountain. Bands who typically performed at the Fillmore had become too big to play the 2,600-seat theater; such groups were now booked into Madison Square Garden and other venues with a larger capacity. For similar reasons, Graham also closed San Francisco's Fillmore West and turned his attention to Winterland and booking major tours. Here, during the New Riders' April 27 set, Garcia seems focused solely on his pedal steel.

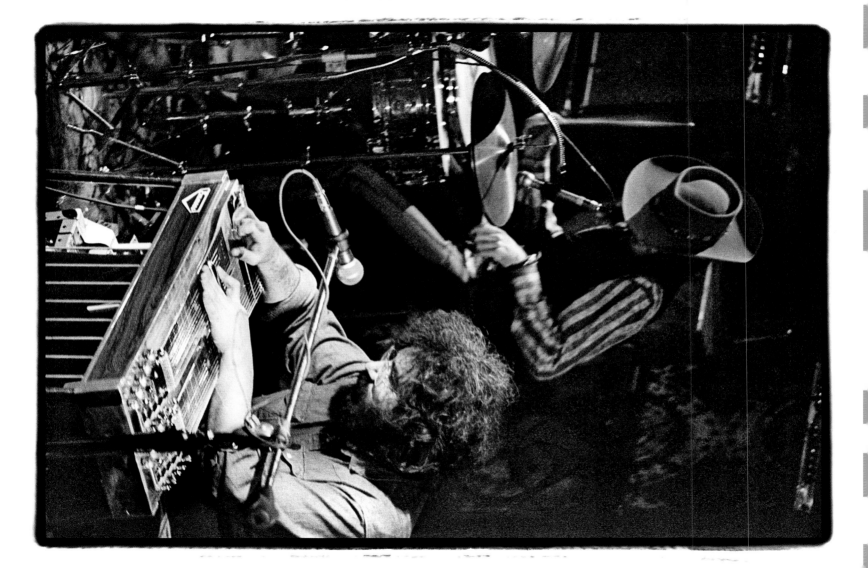

Touring Europe, 1972 painting by Stanley Mouse and Alton Kelley

084

The Dead traveled to Europe for their first tour there on April Fools' Day. As Rock Scully recalled, the trek "was undertaken with the usual alarming casualness. The truly nutty, *demented*, part of it is that the reason this entire venture (monster sound system, twin buses, three-album live set, and ensuing madness) got rolling is because 'some of the dudes in the band wanted to check it out.' *It* being Europe. The Big *It*." Having earned their first gold record in 1971 with the live *Grateful Dead* (aka *Skullfuck*), the band decided to cut another one on the road in Europe. This airbrushed design, along with a Mouse-Kelley painting called *Ice Cream Kid*, would grace the LP jacket.

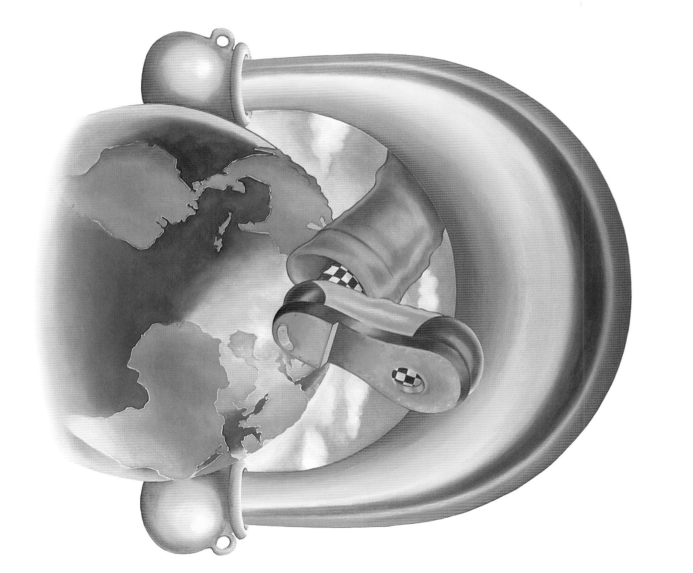

Onstage in Copenhagen, 1972 photograph by Jorgen Angel/Retna

085

After three shows in England, the Dead traveled to Denmark. In Copenhagen they were slated to be filmed for the first-ever live rock & roll broadcast on Danish TV. Unfortunately, roadie Steve Parrish inexplicably knocked out the MC just as he was about to introduce the band. "On the monitor all you see is a big fist coming sideways through the screen, *CRUMP!*" recalls Rock Scully. "Watching this, Jerry doesn't know whether to laugh or cry or tear his hair out." Garcia, who has switched to a Fender from a Gibson to play the band's twangier material, seems to take it all in stride, while Weir is busy with his own fancy fretwork.

Donna Jean Godchaux and Bob Weir, 1972 photograph by Michael Putland/Retna

086

While Pigpen was hospitalized in the fall of '71, a new piano player fell into the band's lap, thanks to Donna Jean Godchaux. A session singer from the famed Muscle Shoals, Alabama, studio, she had moved to San Francisco, met Garcia at a club, and told him about her husband Keith Godchaux's mastery of the keys. Jerry and Keith hit it off, and Keith began playing with the band on October 19 of that year. On occasion, Donna took the mic to harmonize with the band. Once Pigpen returned, there were sometimes seven members onstage. All made the trek to Europe, where this shot was taken.

Garcia and Weir, 1972 photograph by Michael Putland/Retna

087

"Music is something that has optimism built into it. Optimism is another way of saying 'space.' Music has infinite space. You can go as far into music as you can fill millions of lifetimes. Music is an infinite cylinder."

—Jerry Garcia

Jerry Garcia, 1972 photograph by Michael Putland/Retna

088

Increasingly, Jerry Garcia became the spokesman for the Dead, as the band's national popularity escalated following three successful albums. This was not a role he particularly enjoyed. "I'm not the leader of the Grateful Dead or anything like that," he told *Rolling Stone* in 1972. "There isn't any fuckin' leader, I mean, because I can bullshit you guys real easy, but I can't bullshit Phil or Pigpen and them guys watchin' me go through my changes all these years, and we've had so many weird times together. . . . The leader thing doesn't work, because you don't need one."

Ron "Pigpen" McKernan, 1945–1973 photograph by Michael Putland/Retna

089

The European tour, which Pigpen's doctors told him not to attempt, was the last straw for the bluesman's stricken innards; he played his final Dead gig on June 17, 1972, at the Hollywood Bowl. Rather than accompany the band on their fall '72 tour, he stayed home and worked on a solo album. One of the project's songs featured the lyrics "Seems like there's no tomorrow / Seems like all my yesterdays were filled with pain." On March 8, 1973, the twenty-seven-year-old was found dead in his apartment, due to massive internal hemorrhaging. His tombstone reads PIGPEN WAS AND IS NOW FOREVER ONE OF THE GRATEFUL DEAD.

Jerry Garcia, 1973 photograph by Peter Simon/Retna

090

Heartbroken over his buddy's death, Garcia put it this way at Pigpen's funeral: "We can go on calling ourselves the Grateful Dead, but after Pigpen's death we all knew this was the end of the original Grateful Dead." Afterward, Garcia went on as before, spending nearly all his time playing; by 1973, he'd released two side projects (*Hooteroll?*, with Howard Wales in '71, and a solo album in January of '72); performed bluegrass on banjo with Old and In the Way; and issued an LP (*Live at Keystone*) with bassist John Kahn, keyboardist Merl Saunders, and drummer Bill Vitt, all frequent collaborators. Here, Garcia is captured onstage at the Boston Music Hall, where the Dead played November 30 and December 1 and 2.

The Grateful Dead, 1975 photograph by Peter Simon/Retna

091

From October 1974 to June 1976, the Grateful Dead took a hiatus from touring. That didn't stop them from playing—all the members (including Keith and Donna Godchaux) worked on solo projects or various collaborations. The group also got together to perform at a benefit on March 23, 1975, for SNACK (Students Need Athletics, Culture, and Kicks), to aid San Francisco public schools. Joining them onstage were keyboardists Merl Saunders and Ned Lagin. Seen here are Weir, Lagin, Garcia, Lesh, Godchaux, and Saunders (clockwise from left).

Jerry Garcia in Central Park, 1975 photograph by Richard Aaron/Retna

092

In February 1975, the Dead's new self-run label, Round Records, released the live bluegrass album *Old and In the Way*, featuring Garcia on banjo, Peter Rowan on guitar, John Kahn on bass, the legendary Vassar Clements on fiddle, and the album's producer, David Grisman, on mandolin. Garcia found a little bit of country in the city when photographed on April Fools' Day in Central Park.

Blues for Allah, 1975 photograph by Jon Sievert / Getty Images

093

The band reconvened in early '75 at Bob Weir's home studio to begin recording *Blues for Allah*. Inspired by the late king Faisal of Saudi Arabia, the album included liner notes with the title track's lyrics published in Hebrew, Arabic, Persian, and English. (Unfortunately, Garcia had also discovered Persian heroin.) Mickey Hart returned to the fold, adding percussion—and chirping crickets—to the recording, as well as performing with the band. Here, Garcia, Kreutzmann, Lesh, Hart, and Weir (from left), with Phillip Garris's album-jacket artwork peering down behind them.

Bob Weir and Mickey Hart, 1976 photograph by Michael Ochs Archives/Getty Images

094

In June 1976, the Grateful Dead resumed touring. The group scaled back to playing smaller venues and traveling with less crew than they had in the early seventies. Hart was back, and, to protect his ailing vocal cords, Phil Lesh had opted to stop singing. The first song to ring out once the Dead returned to the stage? Bob Weir's "The Music Never Stopped." Here, at San Francisco's Cow Palace, the band revives its New Year's Eve–Bill Graham tradition (for the first time since '72); during the countdown Graham sprang from a giant hourglass.

Phil Lesh, 1976 photograph by Jim Marshall

095

"We used to believe that every place we played was church. But the core of followers is not the reason it feels like church. It's that other thing—[inspiration, grace, transcendence]."

—Phil Lesh

The Grateful Dead in Boston, 1977 photograph by Peter Simon/Retna

096

With the return to the road came a new album, *Terrapin Station*, produced by an outside producer (Keith Olsen) for the first time in eons, and released by the band's new label, Arista. In a 1977 cover story, *Rolling Stone*'s Charles Perry described the band's change of approach: "The Grateful Dead Cadillac of Anarchy—incorporating every hood ornament idea of the counterculture and every electronic gadget—has been traded in for a Grateful Dead Volkswagen of Ecology. So their $450,000 sound system—once one of the seven wonders of rock & roll—has been cannibalized, and they are using (God forbid) a borrowed (from Bill Graham) sound system." Photographed backstage on May 7 at the Boston Garden, the new, lighter Dead: Kreutzmann, Garcia, Weir, Godchaux, Hart, and Lesh (from left), with Donna Jean lying down on the job.

High times, 1977 photograph by Peter Simon/Retna

097 Just prior to their Boston gig, the Dead played a five-night run at New York City's Palladium on East Fourteenth Street (not far from the Fillmore East, which had been turned into a gay disco called The Saint). According to *The Illustrated Trip*, "In the considered opinion of some Deadheads, the spring [1977] tour may have been the band's finest outing of the post-hiatus period." Captured backstage, Garcia, Hart, and Lesh (from left) celebrate at the Palladium.

Bill Kreutzmann at Manor Downs, 1977 photograph by Stephanie Chernikowski

098

On October 12, 1977, under a full moon, the Dead played down the road from Austin, Texas, at an outdoor concert venue operated by Sam Cutler, previously road manager for the Stones and for the Dead. It was unseasonably cold for Texas, but the band managed to make it through, though Bob Weir told the audience his fingers were nearly too frozen to play.

Phil Lesh and fans at Manor Downs, 1977 photograph by Stephanie Chernikowski

Ever since the liner notes to *Skullfuck* had come out with the solicitation "Dead Freaks Unite," encouraging fans to write to "Dead Heads" at the band's office, a growing community had developed around the Grateful Dead. The band kept them posted on concerts, recordings, and general news, and the Dead enthusiasts kept up with one another, many traveling together from town to town to see the band. Here, a few fans hang with Lesh following the Lone Star show.

Jerry Garcia, 1977 photograph by Jim Marshall

100

In November 1977, Jim Marshall photographed Jerry Garcia for the cover of *BAM* (Bay Area Music) magazine. "We've chosen to go with the thing of we don't care whether [audience members] have expectations or not," Garcia once said. "We do what we want to do anyway, because . . . what's in it for us otherwise? We don't want to be entertainers. We want to play music."

Giants Stadium, 1978 photograph by Bob Leafe

101

On Saturday, September 2, 1978, the Dead played Giants Stadium in Rutherford, New Jersey—a much larger venue than they'd been playing. Rumor had it that the moneymaker was to help finance their dream trip to Egypt a few days later. Also on the bill were New Riders of the Purple Sage and Willie Nelson, who brought the Deadhead spirit to country music via that genre's Outlaw movement.

Donna Jean and Jerry onstage in Jersey, 1978 photograph by Jay Blakesberg

102

This shot was the beginning of thirty years (to date) of Jay Blakesburg's photographs featuring Grateful Dead members. Only sixteen years old, Blakesberg was a budding Deadhead. "It was my second annual Labor Day trek—the first being Englishtown the previous year, my first Dead show," he recalls. "It was the beginning of my senior year in high school. I borrowed my father's old Pentax camera and we got a spot on the field maybe forty or fifty feet from the stage. It was a really high stage and they had these giant monitors that blocked nearly everything. In my photos you can only see Jerry from about the chest up, but they're my first shots of the Grateful Dead. By the time I graduated high school, with a Skull and Roses patch hand-sewn to my blue graduation gown, my life was changed. I might not have known it right then and there, but two very pivotal things had happened to me—psychedelics and the Grateful Dead."

Dead in Egypt, 1978 silkscreen by Stanley Mouse

103

For a decade, the Grateful Dead had talked of performing in Egypt by the Great Pyramids. They became the first rock band to put on a show there, with the five-thousand-year-old tomb of Pharaoh Cheops providing an echo chamber for the shows. The first of three nights of gigs took place at the Sound and Light Amphitheater. Before the second night's sets, a Merry Prankster scaled the Great Pyramid and rigged a Dead banner at the top. The final night, all agreed, was best, when the band played during a lunar eclipse. "[It] was one of the great experiences of my life," Bill Graham later expressed, "dancing to 'Sugar Magnolia' in front of the Sphinx and the Great Pyramid."

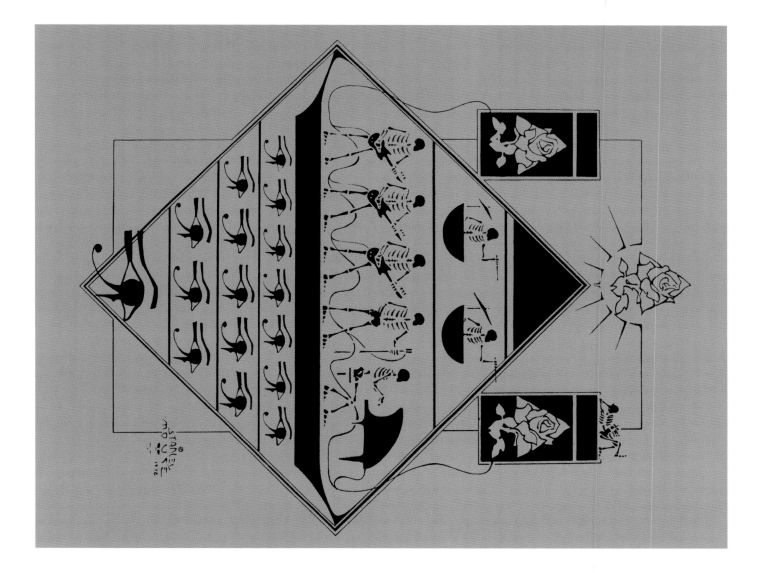

Jerry Garcia out for a ride in Egypt, 1978 photograph by Adrian Boot/Retna

104

As the moon waxed to full, then eclipsed on the Dead's third night at the amphitheater, Graham, Ken Kesey, assorted Pranksters, and Owsley Stanley watched as the band experienced a new high. "I think I kind of left my little reality at [one] point," Bob Weir said after the lunar eclipse performance. "It was so surreal that I wouldn't even try to describe what went through my mind." Communing with a camel apparently popped into Garcia's.

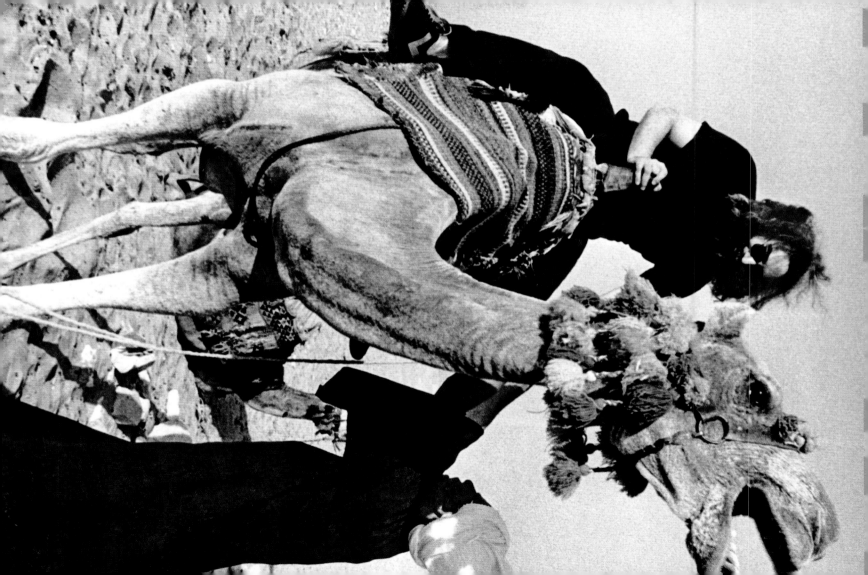

Peekaboo: Godchaux, Garcia, Weir, Lesh, and Hart, 1978

photograph by Richard McCaffrey/Getty Images

105

"Bob and I once set up a formula to deal with interviewers: Depending on how the question was phrased, not the content, you would answer yes or no. It's not uncommon for me to say things that aren't true. Honesty right now has nothing to do with ultimate truth. That's why I try to leave a lot of possibilities for different interpretations in my lyrics. People can fill in their own ideas and make new connections. There's a greater level of participation."

—Jerry Garcia

The Dead at the Capitol Theatre, 1978 photograph by Jay Blakesberg

106

On November 24, 1978 (the day after Thanksgiving), the Dead played an intimate show at the Capitol Theatre, in Passaic, New Jersey. The much-anticipated gig sold out and was broadcast live nationwide. Unfortunately, Garcia had come down with the flu, and he had become increasingly dependent on heroin. Garcia "could barely sing," remembers Blakesberg. "He was incredibly sick. It was just a horrible, horrible show—my first bad Dead show. But I got some really good pictures. It was my first effort to really shoot the band."

Hart, Lesh, and Godchaux, 1978 photograph by Jay Blakesberg

107

Released just in time for this November 24, 1978, gig at the Capitol Theatre was *Shakedown Street*, produced by Little Feat auteur Lowell George. Earlier in the month, on the eleventh, the Dead had played on *Saturday Night Live* for the first time. Apparently, John Belushi, dressed for a skit as Elizabeth Taylor, stopped by the band's dressing room just before its set and joked, "You can do it—you're only performing before *60 million people*."

Give the drummers some, 1978 photograph by Jay Blakesberg

108

Here, Blakesberg managed a rare portrait of Bill Kreutzmann and Mickey Hart in action at the Capitol Theatre. One of the great rituals of a Dead show was their drum duet. That year, Francis Ford Coppola commissioned Hart to create a percussion soundtrack for *Apocalypse Now*. "In the beginning was noise," Hart wrote in his first book, *Drumming at the Edge of Magic*. "And noise begat rhythm, and rhythm begat everything else."

Bob Weir at Madison Square Garden, 1979 photograph by Stephanie Chernikowski

109

For the first time, on January 7 and 8, 1979, the Dead played Madison Square Garden, where they'd eventually rack up a total of fifty-two shows. They had just put on a farewell performance at Bill Graham's Winterland, their final New Year's Eve show there. When asking the band to play, Graham said, "The bulk of the space in my musical memory tank is taken up by my memories of my involvement with the Grateful Dead."

Jerry Garcia at Madison Square Garden, 1979 photograph by Stephanie Chernikowski

110

The Village Voice assigned Stephanie Chernikowski to shoot the Grateful Dead at Madison Square Garden. Both Jerry Garcia and Keith Godchaux wore shades during the Garden concert—reportedly both were grappling with drug addiction at the time. Garcia's preference was Persian Base, a pure, smokable form of heroin.

Keith Godchaux and Phil Lesh at Madison Square Garden, 1979

photograph by Stephanie Chernikowski

About a month after the Garden shows, Godchaux and the Dead would mutually agree
that Keith should leave the band. His marriage to Donna Jean had become rocky,
and his drug addiction had rendered him incapable of handling his keyboard duties.

Bob Weir and Donna Jean Godchaux at Madison Square Garden, 1979

photograph by Stephanie Chernikowski

112

Less than two weeks after the Garden shows, Donna Jean suddenly left the tour. "As a whole, in general, the Grateful Dead is not benign," she later said. Weir contended, "We got into sort of a static situation with Keith and Donna, where we were pretty much locked into this old format."

Keith Godchaux, 1948–1980 photograph by Jon Sievert/Getty Images

113

In July 1980, Keith Godchaux wrecked his car in Marin County. After remaining in a coma for two days, he passed away. Seemingly, following the death of Pigpen, there was a curse on Grateful Dead keyboard players.

Brent Mydland, 1979 photograph by Jay Blakesberg

114

Bob Weir had been playing with keyboardist/vocalist Brent Mydland in his side band, and Jerry Garcia liked Mydland's style. A former band member of Batdorf and Rodney and of Silver, Mydland began rehearsing with the Dead in March and played his first gig with the group on April 22, 1979. Blakesberg took this portrait when he bumped into Weir and Mydland at a No Nukes rally in Washington, DC, on May 7. "I was just walking around the rally and found a press pass lying on the ground," recalls Blakesberg, who was just about to graduate from high school. "I picked it up, pinned it on, and I went backstage and all of a sudden I see Bob Weir and Brent Mydland, who had just joined the band—he'd only played four shows with them at that point. They were just hanging out—they didn't play or anything—and since I was there, I shot ten or fifteen frames. It was my first encounter with a band member. *Relix* [magazine] ran one of the pictures of Brent really big, and that became the first photo a lot of Deadheads had seen of Brent."

The Grateful Dead, 1979 photograph by Herb Greene/Glenn A. Baker Archives/Redferns/Retna

115

About a year after this new band photo was taken, Bob Weir told Ben Fong-Torres for *Rolling Stone*, "We're just now starting to loosen up to the point where we were in 1970, '72, where we can start drifting from key to key, from rhythm to rhythm, and in the jams, some interesting stuff has come up. Once again, we're tending to go to new places every night." Looking lively, Garcia, Weir, Mydland, Lesh, Kreutzmann, and Hart (from left).

Jerry Garcia, Clive Davis, and Robert Klein, 1979 photograph by Ebet Roberts

116

On Thursday, May 10, 1979, Jerry Garcia and the Dead's label head, Clive Davis, sat down with host Robert Klein for his weekly syndicated radio show, recorded at RCA Studios in New York City. The Grateful Dead had played Binghamton, New York, the night before. Six months earlier, Arista had released *Shakedown Street*, which received some of the worst reviews of the band's career, due to its commercial, discoesque sheen.

The Grateful Dead at Madison Square Garden, 1979 photograph by Jay Blakesberg

117

For the third time, the Dead played a sold-out run at Madison Square Garden on September 4–6, 1979. From the audience, then fledgling photographer Jay Blakesberg shot the band with the new camera, complete with zoom lens, that he'd gotten for his eighteenth birthday. "At this point it was a big deal because the Dead were coming and playing Madison Square Garden," Blakesberg recalls. "It was only a couple years earlier that they were still a theater band." Also in the audience were undercover cops (clad in yellow tie-dyed T-shirts) to protect Jerry Garcia, who'd received a death threat prior to the shows. Caught by Blakesberg's lens, Kreutzmann, Garcia, Weir, Hart, and Lesh (from left).

Bob Weir and Phil Lesh at the Oakland Auditorium, 1979

photograph by Jay Blakesberg

118

"That was my first New Year's Eve show," recalls Blakesberg of the December 26–28, 30–31 run at the Oakland Auditorium in 1979. This marked the beginning of the Grateful Dead's annual multinight New Year's shows in the Bay Area, enabling thousands of Deadheads to get a ticket. "I actually took a Greyhound bus out to California [from New Jersey]," says Blakesberg. The concert seen here, on December 26, "was the very first benefit show the Grateful Dead ever did for SEVA—the Wavy Gravy organization where they provide healthcare for third world countries. Bobby is wearing a SEVA shirt [seen here]." The entire concert can be heard on *Dick's Picks, Volume 5* (1996).

Jerry Garcia at the Oakland Auditorium, 1979 photograph by Jay Blakesberg

119

"The Oakland Auditorium was really a great venue," according to Blakesberg, who took this photo during the December 28, 1979, show. "It was one of the best—my favorite West Coast venue. It held about 7,000 people, it sounded really good, and we had a lot of super-psychedelic, memorable moments at that venue—really, really fun stuff."

Deadheads on New Year's Eve, 1979 photograph by Richard McCaffrey/Getty Images

120

By 1979, thousands of Deadheads were traveling the country to see the band. And Bill Graham made sure that the New Year's Eve run in particular would be an unforgettable event for all in attendance. On this night, he appeared at midnight dressed as a gigantic psychedelic butterfly, emerging from a chrysalis (constructed from van parts) to say good-bye to another decade. On Graham's forty-sixth birthday, spent at a San Diego Dead concert, Bob Weir announced to the crowd that the band had bestowed him with the name Uncle Bobo, as a "term of endearment." Though he hated the name, Graham heard numerous calls of "Uncle Bobo" during the last show of the 1970s.

John Kahn and Jerry Garcia, 1980 photograph by Jay Blakesberg

123

Bassist John Kahn and Jerry Garcia had a long-standing musical relationship that extended back to 1970, when they started jamming together at the Bay Area club the Matrix. They also performed together as a duo and in the combos Old and In the Way, Legion of Mary, and Reconstruction. Through the revolving-door lineup that was the Jerry Garcia Band, Kahn was the sole constant.

John Belushi and Jerry Garcia, 1980 photograph by Jay Blakesberg

124

Since the Dead's debut performance on *Saturday Night Live*, Garcia had become buddies with John Belushi and Dan Akroyd. The *SNL* comics' Blues Brothers combo opened for the Dead at Winterland the last night it was open. When in New York, Garcia frequently partied at the Blues Brothers' private club in Manhattan's Meatpacking District. On Sunday, March 30, Belushi joined the Dead onstage at the Capitol Theatre, in Passaic, New Jersey. Blakesberg recalls that Belushi and Garcia were duetting on "U.S. Blues" when he snapped this picture.

The Grateful Dead on SNL, 1980 photograph by Bob Leafe

125

On April 5, 1980, the Dead appeared on *Saturday Night Live* for the second (and final) time. They performed two songs from their new album *Go to Heaven*, which would be released three weeks later. Here, Weir sings his composition (written with John Perry Barlow) "Saint of Circumstance." But it was Hunter and Garcia's "Alabama Getaway," which kicked off the album, that made a bigger impact on the audience, soon becoming the band's highest charting single (number 68) since "Truckin'."

Live in Alaska, 1980 photograph by Jay Blakesberg

126

On June 19–21, 1980, the Dead played their only shows in Alaska, appearing for three nights at the West High Auditorium in Anchorage. "I was just a kid on the Dead tour," Blakesberg recalls. "It was all about the next show! That June of 1980 I was out of college, and I was basically on tour that whole summer. Everybody was really expecting big, magical things for these solstice shows, but they were just pretty straightforward Grateful Dead concerts. It was great, though, because during the set break, we could all go outside and it was solstice, so around 10:00 or 11:00 at night, it was completely light out. It was one of those cool things to go do, you know?"

Deadheads in Maine, 1980 photograph by Jay Blakesberg

127

The year 1980 marked Blakesberg's fourth Labor Day weekend following the Dead; he'd started it all off in New Jersey at Raceway Park in '77 and Giants Stadium in '78, and had then headed to Rochester, New York, in '79. On this September 6, at the last gig of the band's summer tour, Blakesberg documented his fellow Deadheads frolicking at the state fairgrounds in Lewiston, Maine. "Those were the four big end-of-the-summer shows those four years in a row," says Blakesberg, "and then it stopped after that." The band would not play big Labor Day weekend concerts again for several years.

Live at the Warfield, 1980 photograph by Jay Blakesberg

128

A legendary Dead event was the fifteen-show run the group performed at San Francisco's Warfield Theatre beginning in late September 1980. They kicked off the night with an acoustic set (which they hadn't done since 1971); that was followed by two electric sets. The number fifteen held significance for the band—it had been that many years since they'd formed in 1965. A June gig in Colorado commemorated the fifteenth birthday, but most Deadheads consider the Warfield shows (followed by a Radio City run) the true anniversary celebration. Blakesberg, who flew in from New Jersey for the first three concerts, took this picture on the opening night, September 25.

Bill Graham's butterfly, 1980 photograph by Jay Blakesberg

129

In the lobby of the Warfield hung a replica of promoter Bill Graham in the butterfly costume he'd sported the previous New Year's Eve. The intimate theater, with its 2,400 seats, proved the perfect setting for the Dead's return to acoustic music. Graham had speakers placed in the outer aisles and lobbies so Deadheads doing the "Woodstock sun grope" could dance in these areas, rather than obscure the views of those seated. During the electric sets, says Blakesberg, "there was a lot of dancing out in the hallways, which were decorated from top to bottom like a Grateful Dead museum, with photos on the walls and posters and various memorabilia. For a wide-eyed kid from New Jersey out in California for only the second or third time, it was an amazing experience."

Electric set at the Warfield, 1980 photograph by Jay Blakesberg

130

Recordings from the Warfield shows, as well as subsequent performances at Radio City Music Hall in New York, were later released on two live albums: 1981's *Reckoning*, featuring the acoustic material, and that same year's *Dead Set*, which was electric. Blakesberg grabbed this shot of an electric set on September 27, 1980.

Radio City Music Hall, 1980 photograph by Jay Blakesberg

133

The Dead's run at Manhattan's six-thousand-seat showplace Radio City Music Hall followed a template set at the Warfield, with *Saturday Night Live* writers (and Deadheads) Tom Davis and Al Franken serving as hosts. As for Blakesberg, this is one of the sole shots he took of the historic event. "I went to all eight shows they played at Radio City," the lensman recalled, "but I didn't shoot any of those shows. Because I'd gotten so many great shots at the Warfield, I decided I'd just hang out and dance at the shows, instead of worrying about shooting. I was being a fan—a tripping hippie."

Al Franken and Bill Kreutzmann, 1980 photograph by Peter Simon/Retna

134   Backstage at Radio City Music Hall, Al Franken and Bill Kreutzmann share a moment. For the Halloween show at Radio City, Franken and Davis put on hysterical skits parodying Jerry Lewis's annual Labor Day telethon. For these "Jerry's kids," donations bought a tab of acid and a pair of Dead tickets.

Garcia at Radio City, 1980 photograph by Peter Simon/Retna

135

"I'm the sort of person that will just keep going along until something stops me. . . .
You could go at any moment, so you might as well try and cram as much as you can
possibly get into your life."

—Jerry Garcia

Tom Snyder, Bob Weir, and Jerry Garcia, 1981 photograph by Bob Leafe

136

On May 7, 1981, the Grateful Dead appeared on the NBC television program
Tomorrow with Tom Snyder. At the beginning of the show, Weir and Garcia filled
the guest seats, and Snyder (at left), rather tactlessly, told Garcia he looked
a lot older than Weir. Snyder also expressed his gratitude to the band for playing
acoustically—and quietly—on his show.

Jerry Garcia with Gene Shalit and friend, 1981 photograph by Bob Leafe

139

Backstage before appearing on *Tomorrow with Tom Snyder,* Garcia shares a laugh
with NBC film critic and TV personality Gene Shalit (at left). "I try not to lose
touch with my more youthful self," Garcia told Ben Fong-Torres around this time.
"I still basically don't think of myself much differently than I did when I was about
seventeen. I may have a case of extremely protracted adolescence."

Tom Johnston, Bob Weir, and John Entwistle, 1981 photograph by Ebet Roberts

140

Guests on *The Robert Klein Radio Hour* await the mic: former Doobie Brothers guitarist/vocalist Tom Johnston, Bob Weir, and bassist John Entwistle of the Who (from left). The Dead and the Who performed together in 1981, as they had at the Monterey Pop Festival fourteen years earlier.

Jerry Garcia, 1981 photograph by Dister/Dalle/Retna

141

The Grateful Dead had just toured Europe, performing in England, Scotland, Denmark, Germany, Holland, Spain, and France, when this portrait was taken in November. After the last show of the tour, on October 19, 1981, band members wrote a missive to Garcia, who'd become strung out on heroin: "Dear Sir and Brother, You have been accused of certain high crimes and misdemeanors against the art of music. To wit: playing in your own band; never playing with any dynamics; never listening to what anybody else plays. . . ."

The Dead at Nassau Coliseum, 1982 photograph by Frank White

142

By the early eighties, the Dead's music had spread to a wide range of musicians, including original member of the UK pub-rock scene Graham Parker. Parker recalls how he came to cover Garcia's "Sugaree," many years after borrowing Jerry Garcia's first solo album from a friend back in 1972: "I taped [some of the songs] off the vinyl with whatever crude cassette recording device I had in those days. 'Sugaree' had a sinuously funky guitar part that I enjoyed immensely, and I made a note in my head that—if ever I were to become a professional musician—I would one day cover this tune. Fast-forward to 2001, and I'm in England in the house where I grew up, rummaging through the drawer in my childhood bedroom. Out comes a vomit-colored cassette tape emblazoned with the letters EMI. I popped the cassette into the boom box and there it was, 'Sugaree,' in all its glory. But as I scribbled down the words and messed with the chord sequence on my guitar, the depressing *wah wah wah* of a suddenly malfunctioning tape made me reach for the eject button. As the tape jumped out, so did a tiny cube of grayish foam. I stuffed whatever it was into the cassette and back went the tape into the machine. To my amazement, the song continued, albeit somewhere beyond the third verse. And so I had most of the verses and the chords—good enough for rock & roll—and went on to record the song for my faux country effort, *Your Country*, released in 2004. It took me thirty years, but I got there."

The Dead at the Greek Theatre, 1982 photograph by Jay Blakesberg

143

Each May, the Grateful Dead played a series of shows at the Greek Theatre, on the campus of the University of California, Berkeley (tickets cost twelve dollars). Seen here, Lesh, Weir, and Garcia, on May 23, 1982. The annual Greek Theatre runs became not-to-be-missed shows for Deadheads.

Deadhead bus, 1982 photograph by Jay Blakesberg

144

Parked outside the Frost Amphitheater, at Stanford University, in Palo Alto, California, a Deadhead bus awaits its passengers before traveling on to the next show. Much like the Merry Pranksters and driver Neal Cassady with their bus "Further," Deadheads customized their vehicles with psychedelic imagery. Gradually, parking lots at Dead shows would become countercultural bazaars where traveling Deadheads sold such wares as tie-dyed T-shirts to raise the funds to follow the band on the road.

Jimmy Cliff and Bob Weir, 1982 photograph by Ebet Roberts

145

Bob Weir and reggae great/author of "The Harder They Come" Jimmy Cliff chill out during a press conference (at New York's Plaza Hotel) to announce the impending Jamaica World Music Festival, at which the Dead would play, in Montego Bay. The Dead were longtime reggae fans and incorporated elements of the genre into some of their own sonics. The Jerry Garcia Band would cover "The Harder They Come" during a future stint on Broadway.

Bobby & the Midnites, 1982 photograph by Bob Leafe

146

Bob Weir continued to perform with Bobby & the Midnites when not on the road with the Dead. Here, in an exuberant moment, Weir, drummer Billy Cobham, guitarist Bobby Cochran, and new bassist Alphonso Johnson (from left) perform at the Capitol Theatre, in Passaic, New Jersey. The band released its self-titled debut album near the end of 1981.

Mickey Hart and Sly Dunbar, 1982 photograph by Peter Simon/Retna

147

On November 26, 1982, the Dead performed during the wee hours of the morning at the Jamaica World Music Festival in Montego Bay. Other acts at the fest included Jimmy Cliff, Peter Tosh, the B-52's, and Gladys Knight. Here, Mickey Hart trades tips with half of the great Jamaican *riddim* duo Sly and Robbie.

Drums at the Greek Theatre, 1983 photograph by Susana Millman

148

At this May 15, 1983, performance at Berkeley's Greek Theatre, Bill Kreutzmann and Mickey Hart are joined by percussionist Airto Moreira and vocalist Flora Purim. The band played a three-night run from May 13 to 15. Photographer Susana Millman would meet—and eventually marry—the Dead's publicist, Dennis "Scrib" McNally.

The Dead at the Greek Theatre, 1983 photograph by Larry Hulst/Getty Images

149

By 1983, Phil Lesh (far left), whose vocal cords had finally healed, had begun singing again for the first time since 1974. Brent Mydland (far right) sang as well, with soulful vocals that sounded somewhat like Michael McDonald of the Doobie Brothers. Mydland also contributed his songcraft to the band.

New Year's Eve ticket, 1983 photograph by Jay Blakesberg

150 For this New Year's Eve show the Dead moved to a different Bay Area location—the San Francisco Civic Auditorium. The four-night run took place December 27–28 and 30–31, 1983. On New Year's Eve, Bill Graham sprang from a gigantic globe. Joined by Maria Muldaur and Rick Danko, bassist for the Band—who opened the show—the Dead played three sets.

Nº 1350

BILL GRAHAM PRESENTS

GRATEFUL DEAD

SAN FRANCISCO CIVIC AUDITORIUM
SATURDAY, DECEMBER 31, 1983
"NEW YEARS EVE"
8:00 P.M.

General Admission
$20.00

Bobby & the Midnites, 1984 photograph by Bob Leafe

151

In 1984, Bob Weir's Bobby & the Midnites released their second and final album, *Where the Beat Meets the Street*. Here, Weir and guitarist Bobby Cochran can be seen wowing the crowd at one of their favorite venues, the Capitol Theatre, in Passaic, New Jersey.

Jerry Garcia goes acoustic, 1984 photograph by Susana Millman

152

In November 1984, as a duo, Jerry Garcia and John Kahn performed a series of ten shows on the East Coast. Millman took this shot on November 18 in New York City's Avery Fisher Hall, at Lincoln Center. Sadly, Kahn shared the same taste as Garcia in smokable Persian heroin.

The Dead at the Berkeley Community Theater, 1985 photograph by Susana Millman

153

The Grateful Dead played four nights, March 9–10 and 12–13, 1985, to raise money for the Rex Foundation, which they started in 1983 to honor Rex Jackson, their longtime road manager and crew member who'd been killed in a 1976 car accident. The foundation's goals were "to help secure a healthy environment, promote individuality in the arts, provide support to critical and necessary social services, assist others less fortunate than ourselves, protect the rights of indigenous people and ensure their cultural survival, build a stronger community, and educate children and adults everywhere."

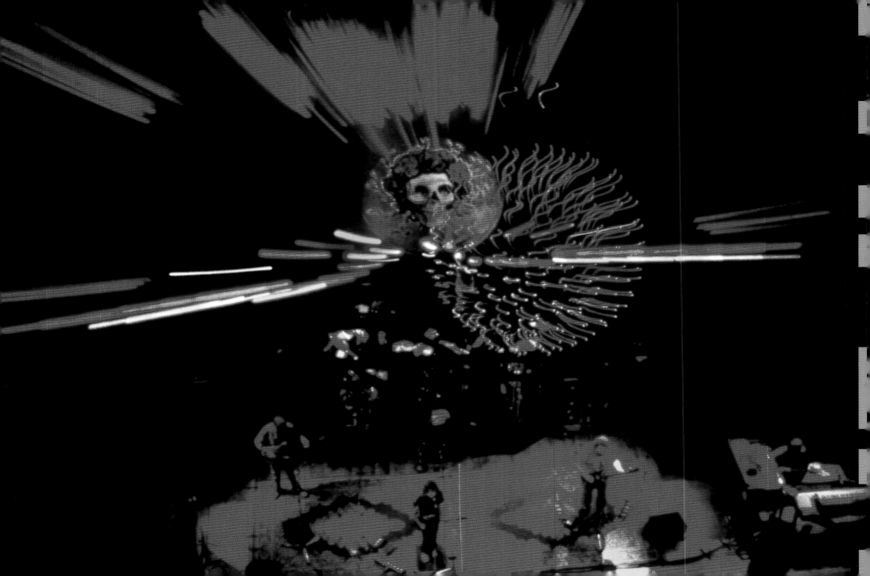

Bob Weir and Carly Simon, 1985 photograph by Peter Simon/Retna

154

Photographer Peter Simon captured his sister Carly engrossed in a song provided by Bob Weir, performed at her New York apartment. Presumably, it was *not* "You're So Vain."

Twentieth-anniversary show, 1985 photograph by Larry Hulst/Getty Images

155

To commemorate their twentieth anniversary as a band, the Dead performed a three-night run June 14–16, 1985, at Berkeley's Greek Theatre. The band's old pal Rick Griffin created a backdrop based on "The Minute Man," Daniel Chester French's 1875 artwork, with a skeleton replacing the Revolutionary War figure. The band held a press conference—only the third in Dead history—to publicize the event. At the Berkeley shows, each concertgoer received a thank-you card, emblazoned with Griffin's design, offering gratitude for "20 years of being an audience that is the envy of every other rock & roll band alive. Fuck 'em if they can't take a joke!"

New Year's Eve, 1985 photograph by Jay Blakesberg

156 Bill Graham, seen here at the Oakland Coliseum Arena dressed as Father Time (center), loved being part of the Dead's festive New Year's Eve celebrations. Each year he tried to outdo himself by arriving onstage in a variety of contraptions.

Deadheads in Berkeley, 1986 photograph by Jay Blakesberg

159

"The magazine that really should write about Deadheads is *National Geographic*.
Get some of those intrepid photogs in their helicopters out here. . . . They'd get
a good shot at some exotic folkways."

—An unnamed Deadhead to Charles Perry for *Rolling Stone*

Deadhead dance, 1986 photograph by Jay Blakesberg

160

"What we stand for, and what we represent to a lot of people, is misfit power."
—Bob Weir

Dylan and the Dead, 1986 photograph by Ebet Roberts

161

It was a perfect coupling: Bob Dylan and the Grateful Dead. Garcia was playing bluegrass, folk, and old-timey music when Dylan was starting his career in the early sixties. Touring in 1986 with Tom Petty and the Heartbreakers, Dylan initially joined forces for a triple-bill, five-show stint with the Dead and the Heartbreakers in June and July. Here, Dylan joins the Dead on "It's All Over Now, Baby Blue" and "Desolation Row" at the scorching-hot RFK Stadium, in Washington, DC, on July 7—Lesh, Dylan, Weir, and Garcia (from left). Three days later, Garcia collapsed at home and was rushed to the hospital, where he went in and out of a coma for four days. When he finally awoke, he uttered the words "I'm not Beethoven."

Bob Weir, 1986 photograph by Susana Millman

162

Throughout September 1986, while Garcia continued to struggle to recover both physically and mentally from his ordeal, healing rituals were held for him in various locations. Merl Saunders helped Garcia relearn how to play guitar. The same month, Bob Weir played this acoustic solo show in northern California, at the San Gregorio Music Festival.

Deadheadmobile, 1986 photograph by Jay Blakesberg

163

After getting his feet wet doing a few Jerry Garcia Band shows and guest appearances, Garcia finally reunited with the Dead for a jubilant three-date run at the Henry J. Kaiser Convention Center beginning on December 15. Slimmer and more robust, he thrilled the crowd on opening night, kicking off with "Touch of Grey." The New Year's Eve run went on as planned less than two weeks later. Parked outside was this car, emblazoned with SEE YA NEXT SHOW, which held even more meaning considering Garcia's miraculous return.

Garcia with Santana and friends, 1987 photograph by Jay Blakesberg

164

The year 1987 would become one of the biggest in the Grateful Dead's three-decade-long career. On Sunday, February 15, Garcia, Weir, and Hart participated in a benefit for a Mickey Hart cause, World Music in Schools, with a performance at the Veterans Memorial Auditorium in Petaluma, California. Here, Carlos Santana (back, left) and Garcia can be seen backing up Babatunde Olatunji and his Drums of Passion.

Deadheads on the lawn, 1987 photograph by Jay Blakesberg

165

"We didn't invent our original audience. In a way this whole process has kind of invented us. I don't know why, and I can't say what motivates them. Back in the seventies, we had the same phenomenon of all these young kids. But now those are the people who are in medical school and law school—they are college people and professionals. They still come to shows. So now there are Deadheads every-where. They've kind of infiltrated all of American society—everybody knows one."

—Jerry Garcia

Tie-dye for sale, 1987 photograph by Jay Blakesberg

166

Deadheads were not the only vendors setting up at Dead shows as the 1987 spring tour traveled east. "The parking lot scene in particular was getting out of control," details *The Illustrated Trip*. "Professional T-shirt sellers and other 'merch' vendors out for a fast buck started to outnumber the Tourheads who sold homemade crafts or whole foods for tickets and traveling money." Blakesberg caught this sunny scene on March 1, three weeks before the band embarked on the East Coast tour, at Oakland's Henry J. Kaiser Convention Center.

"Touch of Grey" video shoot, 1987 photograph by Jay Blakesberg

167

During the Dead's May 9–10, 1987, concert at Laguna Seca Raceway, in Monterey, California, director Gary Gutierrez shot footage for the band's first MTV-era video. "Touch of Grey," written in 1982 and the opening track of the Dead's forthcoming album *In the Dark*, had been selected for the honor. The weekend-long concert commemorated the twentieth anniversary of the Monterey Pop Festival, held June 16–18, 1967.

RATEFUL DEAD
ROLL
SCENE
TAKE
C3
108
1
PROD. USFX
DIR. GUTIERREZ CAM. KIKUGAWA
DATE 5-9-87
Earl

Jerry Skellington, 1987 photograph by Jay Blakesberg

168

In addition to filming the band playing "Touch of Grey," director Gutierrez shot life-size puppet skeletons performing the same motions as their human counterparts. Filming took place after the concert, but camping Deadheads volunteered to stick around to serve as the skeletons' cheering audience.

"Touch of Grey" video still, 1987 photograph by Jay Blakesberg

169

On June 16, 1987, Arista released "Touch of Grey" as a single, and the song began to soar up the *Billboard* chart. Twenty-two years into their career, the Grateful Dead finally scored their first bona fide hit single. Three days later, "Touch of Grey" debuted on MTV and quickly spun into heavy rotation. By August, the tune had hit number 9 on the charts, and a whole new generation of Dead fans was born. Longtime Deadheads called this new crop of fans Touchheads.

Laguna Seca Raceway concert, 1987 photograph by Jay Blakesberg

170

On May 9, 1987, a crowd that would soon grow to nearly thirty-five thousand began to gather for the Laguna Seca Dead concert. Opening acts included Ry Cooder and Bruce Hornsby and the Range. Hornsby would eventually become an unofficial member of the Dead. Photog Blakesberg found himself on the other side of the camera when the "Touch of Grey" video was filmed later that night. "I'm the guy in the mullet," he says of his spotlight among audience members. "I didn't want to let go of my long hair just yet! They were doing crowd shots, and all of our friends went in and rushed right to the middle, but I wanted to be over to the left a little because it was a better angle to shoot. I ended up the one who was in the video."

Dancing to the Dead, 1987 photograph by Jay Blakesberg

171

"Our audience tends to be intelligent enough and individualistic enough so that they don't have an easy time fitting into the mainstream in their schools. They're different, and they need refuge—they need a place they can go where they belong. There aren't any initiations or requirements or membership tests or anything else to become a Deadhead; you just have to like it and feel like you're part of it and then you're a brother to them all."

—John Perry Barlow

Jerry Garcia, 1987 photograph by Jay Blakesberg

172

"I am not a believer in the invisible, but I got such an incredible outpouring—the mail I got in the hospital was so soulful. All the Deadheads—it was kind of like brotherly, sisterly, motherly, fatherly advice from people. . . . Every conceivable kind of healing vibe was just pouring into that place. The doctors did what they could to keep me alive, but as far as knowing what was wrong with me and knowing how to fix it—it's not something medicine knows how to do. I really feel the fans put life into me . . . and that feeling reinforced a lot of things. It was like, 'Okay, I've been away for a while, folks, but I'm back!'"

—Jerry Garcia

Bob Weir and Jerry Garcia, 1987 photograph by Jay Blakesberg

173

"The one thing we knew we could do—and found a great deal of satisfaction
doing—was playing live. It wasn't so much an ideal as what was realistic for us at
the moment. That's the medium that works for us. There are people that you're
playing to, that you're getting immediate gratification from, and that's preferable."

—Bob Weir

The Dead onstage at Laguna Seca, 1987 photograph by Susana Millman

174

"In their best moments, the Grateful Dead are still as eloquent and alluring as in their go-for-broke heyday. More remarkably, they still sound like a unit without any fixed center: The melodic focus still shifts somewhere between Jerry Garcia's restive guitar lines and Phil Lesh's nervy bass runs; the rhythmic impulses pull back and forth between Bill Kreutzmann's swinglike tempos and Mickey Hart's edgier attack; and the harmonic action veers between Bob Weir's fitful rhythm guitar chords and keyboardist Brent Mydland's passion for soulful dissonance. . . . In practice, this is the same band that made 'Dark Star' and 'Uncle John's Band' count for so much a generation ago: a band that needs all its members working and thinking together to keep things moving and balanced."

—Mikal Gilmore on the Laguna Seca shows, for *Rolling Stone*

Phil Lesh, 1987 photograph by Jay Blakesberg

175

On June 6, 1987, avant-garde-music aficionado Phil Lesh paid a visit to Berkeley radio station KPFA. Together with Gary Lambert, who served as editor of the *Grateful Dead Almanac*, Lesh hosted a new radio show that featured experimental music, both historical and current. The program, which debuted that day, was called *Eyes of Chaos/Veil of Order*. Lambert invited Blakesberg to stop by, says the photographer. "Phil was kind of goofing off and being playful for the camera, pretending to steal tapes from the station. He was just having fun."

The Alone and Together tour, 1987

photograph by Jay Blakesberg

176

On July 4, 1987, the Grateful Dead and Bob Dylan kicked off a six-stadium tour entitled the Alone and Together tour. Though they had spent a month rehearsing with him prior to the tour, Dylan still managed to pull a number ("Mr. Tambourine Man") out of his hat. He later commented that the Dead "taught me to look inside these songs I was singing . . . actually at the time of that tour, I couldn't even sing. There were so many layers and so much water had gone round that I had a hard time grasping the meaning of them. . . . I realized that they understood those songs better than I did at the time." Here, Lesh, Kreutzmann, Hart, Weir, Dylan, and Garcia (from left) at the Autzen Stadium, in Eugene, Oregon.

Dylan and the Dead, 1987 photograph by Jay Blakesberg

177

"I loved Dylan and the Dead," says Jay Blakesberg. "I thought it was great. Dylan has always been really important to the Grateful Dead songbook, or the Grateful Dead song selection, I should say. The Jerry Garcia Band always did 'Tangled Up in Blue,' and the Dead started playing 'It's All Over Now, Baby Blue.' 'When I Paint My Masterpiece' was a big Jerry Band song, and Dylan songs were always really, really big in the Dead camp. So having Dylan actually sing them with the Dead. . . . Evidently, Dylan loved Jerry." Here, on July 24, 1987, the band stops at the Oakland County Coliseum Stadium, home to the sole performance of "Shelter from the Storm."

The Dead go gold, 1987 photograph by Susana Millman

178

During the five-night sold-out stint at Madison Square Garden, from September 15 to 20, 1987, Arista arranged a little photo op backstage; only two and a half months after its release, *In the Dark* had gone gold (it would eventually go platinum). *The New York Times* pop critic Jon Pareles said of the album, "The best Dead songs do something most rock doesn't even attempt. Like old-time mountain music and blues, they stare death, bad luck, and metaphysical demons in the eye, then shrug and keep on truckin'." As for label boss Clive Davis, he was baffled that "Touch of Grey" was not included in the Garden shows: "I could not believe that they could have a set during the life of this single that did not include the single." Here, looking dubious, are Mydland, Weir, baby Grahame Lesh, Lesh, Kreutzmann, John Cutler (who coproduced the album with Garcia), Garcia, and Hart (from left).

Harry Popick, 1987 photograph by Susana Millman

179

Crew member Harry Popick—the monitor mixer on the road—played one of the devils in the Grateful Dead video of "Hell in a Bucket," written by Bob Weir, John Perry Barlow, and Brent Mydland. The song was featured on a twelve-inch promotional single released in September, which was followed by the short-form-video version.

She-devils, 1987 photograph by Susana Millman

180

Grateful Dead family and office staff were recruited to play the "Hell in a Bucket" she-devils in the video: Mary Jo Meinolf, Eileen Law, Sue Stephens, Jerry's daughter Teresa "Trixie" Garcia, Janet Soto-Knudsen, Diane Geoppo, Frances Shurtliff, Basia Raizene, Nancy Mallonee, Maruska Nelson, and (partially obscured) manager Jon McIntire (from left).

"Hell in a Bucket" scene, 1987 photograph by Susana Millman

181

Garcia and Weir star alongside a duck in this scene from "Hell in a Bucket," shot at New George's Bar in San Rafael, California. "Weir has always been a sharing kind of guy," quips Millman, "and there were no laws about getting ducks drunk back in the eighties." That fall, the band also released *So Far*, a fifty-five-minute video that mixed live concert footage with animation.

Garcia and Tiger, 1987 photograph by Jay Blakesberg

182

Garcia had started performing with the photogenic guitar he called Tiger back in 1979; here he plays it at Bill Graham's new twenty-two-thousand-seat venue the Shoreline Amphitheatre in Mountain View, California. Blakesberg captured a sublime Garcia: "For me, it was about waiting, waiting, waiting," he relates, "and capturing that magical moment in that split second where it all came out—whether it was a combination of the lighting, the emotion from the artist, the facial expression."

"Throwing Stones" video, 1987 photograph by Jay Blakesberg

185

On November 5, 1987, the Dead and a film crew converged on an abandoned school yard in Oakland to make a video for "Throwing Stones." (Bill Kreutzmann was absent that day, but Robbie Taylor, a member of the road crew, wore a mask and acted as his stand-in.) In quintessential Deadlike serendipity, the event turned into a dream photo shoot for Blakesberg, who happened to live across the street from the location, where a mural was painted to serve as the backdrop: "I had been shooting a lot for *Relix* [magazine, where J. C. Juanis] seemed to have his finger on the pulse. We'd been hearing that this shoot was going to happen. . . . When I got the call from J. C., I just showed up. I hadn't met Dennis McNally at that point, and I remember Garcia asking McNally who I was, and McNally says to me, 'Jerry was asking, "What's your name again?"' and I said, 'Jay Blakesberg, *Relix* magazine.' We'd never cleared it with him or asked permission, but I was already there shooting so he probably just assumed I belonged there and never really questioned it. I'm sure in hindsight, if they'd checked it out carefully, they would've kicked my ass right out of there. It did end up being a big spread in *Relix*."

"Throwing Stones" shoot, 1987 photograph by Jay Blakesberg

186

"The band wore these costumes—these big Australian oil coats [dusters]—that were pretty cool," remembers Blakesberg of the video shoot. "They seemed to enjoy wearing the funky clothes and wearing the big hats—it was something they never did."

Brent Mydland and daughter, 1987 photograph by Jay Blakesberg

187

Though Brent Mydland had been with the Dead for eight years, he still considered himself the "new guy." He rarely gave interviews and suffered from depressive mood swings. Though he contributed to the band's most commercially successful albums both in songwriting and vocals, the keyboardist still felt insecure, according to Dead biographer and former publicist Dennis McNally. Among his compositions were "Just a Little Light" (written with Barlow) and "I Will Take You Home," a lullaby for his daughters, two of the four Mydland songs that would appear on 1989's *Built to Last*.

Jerry Garcia, 1987 photograph by Jay Blakesberg

188

At the end of the video shoot, a guy from the crew approached Garcia and asked him to hold a sign reading HAPPY NEW YEAR, so he could use it for his Christmas card. Unbelievably, Garcia complied—though he took off his hat and duster and put on a rather forlorn expression. Here, still dressed as a Western hero, Garcia takes a cigarette break.

Mickey Hart, 1987 photograph by Jay Blakesberg

189

All the band members were feeling loose and friendly while, ironically, shooting
a video—"Throwing Stones"— about the world's ills. Never underestimate
the power of dressing like a cowboy! Mickey Hart discovered some old graffiti
on the schoolhouse wall with a tag and a depiction of his last name. He grabbed
Blakesberg and told him, "Take a picture of me with the heart!"

Jerry Garcia and his Takamine, 1987 photograph by Jay Blakesberg

190

On December 17, 1987, Garcia, Weir, and bassist John Kahn formed an acoustic ensemble to perform at an event billed as Joan Baez and Friends: A Christmas Concert. An AIDS benefit held at the Warfield, the occasion found the trio performing "When I Paint My Masterpiece," "Deep Elem Blues," "Victim or the Crime," and "Bird Song." They backed up Baez on "Knockin' on Heaven's Door" and two other numbers.

Jerry Garcia and Carlos Santana, 1988 photograph by Jay Blakesberg

191

Bill Graham organized a benefit to aid the people of El Salvador on January 23, 1988, at the Henry J. Kaiser Convention Center in Oakland. Among the participants, Jerry Garcia and Carlos Santana (seen here in Santana's dressing room) formed a "supergroup" with Bob Weir, Chester Thompson, and the Tower of Power horn section. Also performing were NRBQ, Randy Jackson (future *American Idol* judge), Bonnie Raitt, and Wayne Shorter.

Bob Weir, Bill Graham, and Jerry Garcia, 1988 photograph by Jay Blakesberg

192

"This was one of my very first assignments for *Rolling Stone*," Blakesberg recalls of this portrait. "I had seen Jerry walk into that dressing room and I just kind of walked in, and McNally was standing there and I looked at him and said, 'Can I get a couple of shots?' and he looked at those guys and said, 'Can he get a couple of shots?' and they were like, 'Yeah,' and I just went *click, click, click, click* and shot a series of images and walked out. That's why [*Rolling Stone* photo editor] Jodi Peckman loved me—because I wasn't afraid to walk into Jerry's dressing room!"

Mardi Gras, 1988 photograph by Susana Millman

193

The Grateful Dead brought a little New Orleans to San Francisco with their Mardi Gras shows; this one occurred on February 16, 1988, at the Henry J. Kaiser Convention Center. Millman took the festive shot during the parade of costumed Deadheads, which began with the second set, while the band played the Big Easy favorite "Iko Iko."

Brent Mydland, 1988 photograph by Jay Blakesberg

196

On May 1, 1988, the band played a favorite venue, the Frost Amphitheater. "It's an outdoor venue on the campus of Stanford," explains Blakesberg. "It was a favorite place of Deadheads because it was this sloping grass amphitheater that held about 6,000 or 7,000 people. It was a really great place to see the band. The sound was great, outdoors." Here, Mydland sings one of his emotive ballads.

Dennis McNally, Dick Latvala, and John Taber, 1988 photograph by Susana Millman

197 Three of the Dead family—publicist Dennis "Scrib" McNally; archivist and namesake of *Dick's Picks* Dick Latvala; and Bill Graham Presents dressing-room security guard John Taber—hang backstage at Berkeley's Greek Theatre on July 15, 1988. When the Dead renegotiated a new record deal with Arista after the success of "Touch of Grey," they got the rights to release their live archival recordings themselves, hence the genesis of *Dick's Picks*. McNally would go on to write the essential biography of the Grateful Dead, *A Long Strange Trip*, which he dedicated to Latvala and Garcia.

Jerry Garcia with Zero at Golden Gate Park, 1988 photograph by Jay Blakesberg

198

On the afternoon of July 16, 1988, before playing a Greek Theatre gig later that evening, Garcia joined the band Zero, featuring old pal Merl Saunders and Pete Sears, at a rally in support of the US/USSR Peace Walk. The gathering was organized to celebrate the efforts of a group of antiwar activists who set out to walk from San Francisco to Washington, DC.

Jerry Garcia with Zero, 1988 photograph by Jay Blakesberg

199

"This was in the Golden Gate Park band shell," says Blakesberg. "Jerry came and played a couple of songs with these guys and then left. Zero was a band that [former Quicksilver Messenger Service guitarist] John Cipollina [at left] started with a guitarist named Steve Kimock [at right] and some other people. That was kind of like the house band for the benefit, and Jerry sat in with them."

David Byrne and Bob Weir, 1988 photograph by Susana Millman

200

Talking Heads cofounder and world-music enthusiast David Byrne was an unlikely Deadhead but frequently sang the praises of the band. Here, he hangs with Weir at the Greek Theatre show on July 16, 1988; Byrne was interviewed for a radio broadcast by Dead scholar David Gans, who asked him if it was true that the Talking Heads were the Grateful Dead of the eighties, to which Weir quipped, "God help 'em!" The Tom Tom Club, formed by Talking Heads bassist Tina Weymouth and drummer Chris Frantz, would open for the Dead that New Year's Eve.

Suzanne Vega and Jerry Garcia, 1988 photograph by Ebet Roberts

201

In September 1988, the Dead performed one of the longest run of shows in their career—nine concerts over eleven days at Madison Square Garden. During the final performance, on September 24, they were joined onstage by numerous guests. The second set featured Suzanne Vega, backed by the Dead; she sang "Chinese Bones" by UK singer-songwriter (and former Soft Boy) Robyn Hitchcock, as well as her original "Neighborhood Girls."

Jerry Garcia and Mick Taylor, 1988 photograph by Ebet Roberts

202

Former Rolling Stones guitarist Mick Taylor joined the Dead during the first set of the September 24, 1988, performance at the Garden. The Dead donated the proceeds of the final show to Greenpeace, Cultural Survival, and the Rainforest Action Network. "This, we feel, is an issue strong enough and life-threatening enough . . . ," said Garcia at a press conference. "We want to see the world survive to play games, even if they're atrocious." The concert netted more than $600,000 toward the rainforest-preservation effort.

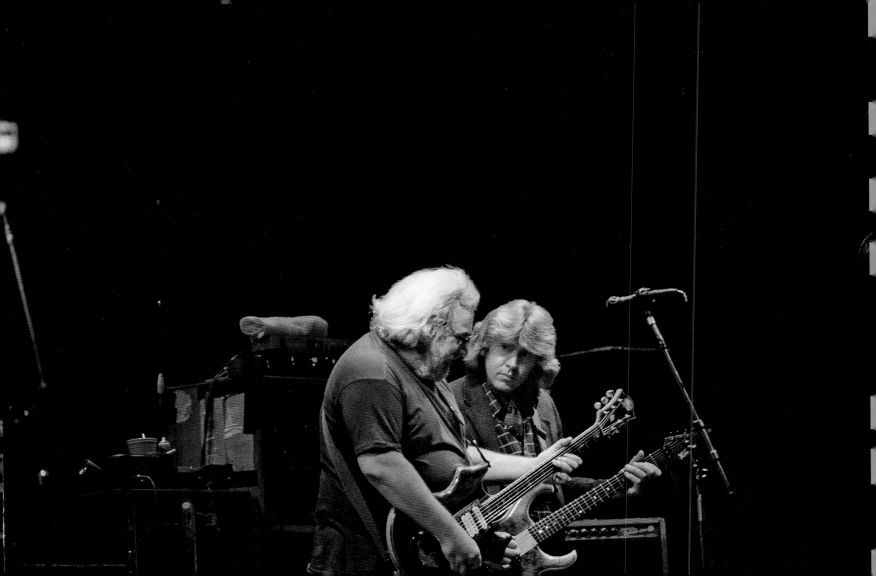

Jerry Garcia, 1989 photograph by Susana Millman

203

"Success has never been part of our schedule, exactly. It's kind of been a happy surprise, but in a way it presents itself as just a new level of problems. And not that it's not gratifying—it's gratifying to have an audience. For us, it's been slow and steady enough where none of it has been a shock."

—Jerry Garcia to Fred Goodman for *Rolling Stone*

Mardi Gras show, 1989 photograph by Jay Blakesberg

204

On Tuesday, February 7, 1989, the Dead played their annual Mardi Gras gig at the Henry J. Kaiser Convention Center in Oakland. The day before, the band did the Chinese New Year show. Also in February, Columbia released the album *Dylan & the Dead*, which documented performances from their 1987 tour together. Dylan selected the album's tracks.

Jerry Garcia and Mickey Hart, 1989 photograph by Jay Blakesberg

205

On March 22, 1989, the band held a press conference at the Fillmore Auditorium
to announce an upcoming benefit concert to raise money for AIDS research. Also
in attendance was Huey Lewis. That night, Garcia, Bob Weir, and John Kahn would
perform as an acoustic trio to benefit a group called Artists Rights Today. The
organization was formed to help poster artists—including the "Big Five" who had
created Family Dog and Fillmore handbills—receive their legal and financial due
for their previous work.

Jerry Garcia and Elvis Costello, 1989 photograph by Jay Blakesberg

206

John Goddard's Village Music was a favorite Mill Valley record store that held anniversary gatherings every year at the nearby club Sweetwater. About seventy-five people gathered for this one on April 24, 1989, including Deadhead Elvis Costello. Around this time, Costello was known to pull out "Stella Blue" and "Ship of Fools" in his set. Here, Jerry Garcia is playing Costello's Fender Jazzmaster while Costello goes acoustic. Also onstage were Bob Weir and Sammy Hagar, as well as Garcia's idol, James Burton, who'd played guitar with fallen heroes Ricky Nelson, Elvis Presley, and Gram Parsons. (Sadly, Village Music closed in late 2007.)

Bob Weir and Jerry Garcia, 1989 photograph by Jay Blakesberg

207

On Saturday, May 6, 1989, the Dead play the first of a two-day final run at one of their favorite venues, the Frost Amphitheater, at Stanford University in Palo Alto, California. Alas, the group's audience had grown so dramatically that it was forced to perform at larger venues than the Frost.

The Grateful Dead's last weekend at the Frost Amphitheater, 1989

photograph by Jay Blakesberg

208

With Stanley Mouse and Alton Kelley's jester painting hanging overhead, the Dead say farewell to a special venue. At the Frost, Phil Lesh, Bill Kreutzmann, Bob Weir, Mickey Hart, Jerry Garcia, and Brent Mydland (from left).

Jester backdrop, 1989 photograph by Tim Mosenfelder/Getty Images

The Mouse/Kelley jester image made an early appearance on the 1972 *Grateful Dead Songbook*, then dressed solely in green. Here, the jester looks to be attired for a Mardi Gras celebration. Yet another rendering graces the cover of Rock Scully's memoir *Living with the Dead*—a Mouse painting of the jester facing the sinking sun, instrument in hand.

The Black & White Ball, 1989 photograph by Jay Blakesberg

210

Numerous Bay Area musicians and visiting pals turned up for the annual Black
& White Ball, benefiting the San Francisco Symphony. Here, on May 12, 1989,
Narada Michael Walden, E Street Band member Clarence Clemons, Todd
Rundgren, Bob Weir, and Huey Lewis (from left) mug for the camera at the
San Francisco Civic Center.

Jerry Garcia and John Fogerty, 1989 photograph by Jay Blakesberg

211

On May 27, 1989, the Grateful Dead participated in the star-studded benefit In Concert Against AIDS, at the Oakland Coliseum Arena. Jerry Garcia and Bob Weir backed up John Fogerty, who, due to a lawsuit with his former band's record label, usually refused to play any Creedence Clearwater Revival songs at the time. Clarence Clemons joined the Dead onstage for their set. Tragically, two days later, the Dead's old buddy John Cipollina, Quicksilver Messenger Service guitarist, would die from a respiratory ailment at age forty-six.

Cesar Rosas of Los Lobos and Jerry Garcia, 1989 photograph by Jay Blakesberg

212

Also participating in the AIDS benefit at Oakland Coliseum Arena was Los Lobos. The East LA group had become a favorite of Jerry Garcia's, and to this day the blues-loving road warriors jam on a Dead-tinged version of "Not Fade Away," a highlight of their concerts. Here, guitarist/vocalist Cesar Rosas poses with Jerry Garcia backstage.

AIDS benefit photo op, 1989 photograph by Jay Blakesberg

213

Promoter Bill Graham (far right) organized the May 27, 1989, AIDS benefit. Here, he poses with Jerry Garcia, Bob Weir, Steve Jordan (drummer for Eric Clapton and others), John Fogerty, and bassist Randy Jackson. Horribly, Graham would be killed in a helicopter accident two years later, on October 25, 1991.

Jerry Garcia, 1989 photograph by Jay Blakesberg

214

"I really love [Jerry's] playing—it's very lyrical, humorous, and unpredictable. I like his use of harmonics, and the endless modulations he goes through. But my favorite thing is that sense of fearlessness."

—Elvis Costello

Bob Weir and Jerry Garcia at Giants Stadium, 1989

photograph by Michael Uhll/Ebet Roberts Archives

215

On July 9 and 10, 1989, the Grateful Dead played Giants Stadium, in East Rutherford, New Jersey. Los Lobos opened this show, on the ninth; the Neville Brothers opened the following night. To kick things off, while tuning up, the Dead regaled the crowd with a snippet from the *Addams Family* theme song. As Deadhead and radio DJ Rick Schneider points out about the band, "They were the MCs of the world's ultimate party."

Giants Stadium crowd, 1989 photograph by Michael Uhll/Ebet Roberts Archives

216

In advance of the '89 summer tour, a mailing was sent out to Deadheads, with the following proposal: "We gratefully invite you to experience the unexpected era of Mega Dead-dom. Take it with the grain of salt it deserves and enjoy watching the ripples as our personal tributary begins mingling with larger currents. It's just as weird for us as it is for you, but, after all, this wasn't meant to be a private party!"

Blame it on Jerry, 1989 photograph by Susana Millman

217

When the Dead performed at the Cal Expo Amphitheatre in Sacramento, California, Jerry Garcia and Bob Weir participated in an impromptu press conference and photo op. "Someone gave Jerry this sticker," Susana Millman recalls, "which had been floating around for years. Here he shows his usual modest pride."

Greek Theatre farewell, 1989 photograph by Susana Millman

218

Also falling victim to the Grateful Dead's exploding fan base were their beloved Greek Theatre runs. The band performed at the bowl-shaped Berkeley amphitheater twenty-nine times between 1980 and 1989. Three Rex Foundation benefits marked the Dead's final appearances at the Greek, from August 17 to 19. Here, during the final show, are Bill Kreutzmann, Bob Weir, Mickey Hart, and Jerry Garcia (from left).

Jerry at WNEW, 1989 photograph by Ebet Roberts

221

On October 16, 1989, Jerry Garcia paid a visit to legendary New York City DJ Scott Muni, who spun discs at what was then Manhattan's top rock radio station. The band was in the midst of performing five nights—October 11–12, and 14–16—at the Brendan Byrne Arena, aka the Meadowlands, in East Rutherford, New Jersey. Speaking on Muni's radio show, Garcia hinted that the Dead would play "Dark Star" that night. The same day, a horse named Dark Star placed at the Meadowlands Racetrack, and indeed, much to Deadheads' delight, the band jammed on the eponymous tune that final night of the run.

Rob Wasserman and Bob Weir, 1989 photograph by Jay Blakesberg

222 Bassist Rob Wasserman and guitarist Bob Weir performed as a duo and opened up some shows for the Jerry Garcia Band throughout 1989, including at the Open Air Theater, in San Diego, and at the Irvine Meadows Amphitheatre, in Irvine.

Rob Wasserman, Edie Brickell, and Jerry Garcia, 1990 photograph by Jay Blakesberg

223

Lead vocalist of New Bohemians (and future wife of Paul Simon) Edie Brickell joined Rob Wasserman and Jerry Garcia in the studio on January 4, 1990. Their improvisational recordings would eventually be released on Wasserman's 1994 album *Trios*. "It was interesting to see Jerry around someone like Edie Brickell, who was very big at the time," Jay Blakesberg recalls. "Jerry was like a teenager on a first date around her." Years later, Blakesberg presented this photo as a gift to Paul Simon, who was thrilled with the shot of his wife flanked by Garcia and Wasserman.

Mardi Gras, 1990 photograph by Jay Blakesberg

224

On February 27, 1990, the Dead played their customary Mardi Gras performance at the Oakland Coliseum Arena. The third of three nights, this gig featured the opening act—courtesy of Louisiana—Michael Doucet and Beausoleil, who also joined the Dead on "Iko Iko" and "Man Smart, Woman Smarter." According to *The Illustrated Trip*, "Each year the Fat Tuesday parades became more and more elaborate, incorporating huge papier-mâché figures and trippy Dead-related floats."

Bob Weir, Jerry Garcia, and Brent Mydland, 1990 photograph by Jay Blakesberg

225

"No matter what anybody says, the Grateful Dead were punk as fuck. Pirates, wild men. Doing huge-ass shows regardless of mainstream cred."

—Ryan Adams

Buck Henry and Mickey Hart, 1990 photograph by Susana Millman

226

On June 17, 1990, while the band played a three-day run at the Shoreline Amphitheatre in Mountain View, California, writer/actor Buck Henry interviewed the Dead for a television special planned on the band. "Alas, it never really came off," Susana Millman reports. But there was other news: As the band performed "Stella Blue," a fan in attendance gave birth to a baby girl who, during the pregnancy, had been christened with the same name.

Bob Weir and Jerry Garcia, 1990 photograph by Jay Blakesberg

227

Weir and Garcia seem to be looking for something, while 22,000 people watch, at the Shoreline Amphitheatre on Sunday, June 16, 1990. Likewise, plenty of Deadheads showed up at concerts looking for tickets. As poet and writer Sparrow recalls, "I believed in going to a sold-out Dead concert clutching $17.50 to see if the Universe wished me to enter. In 1990, a friendly guy sold me an extra ticket, and I walked past thousands of ticket beggars on my way into the concert. I felt like a millionaire strolling through Calcutta. But the Universe had chosen me— didn't they understand?"

Nelson Mandela celebration, 1990

photograph by Jay Blakesberg

228

After Nelson Mandela was released from prison in South Africa, Bill Graham promoted his speaking tour across the United States. Before his appearance at the Oakland Coliseum Arena, members of the Dead, including Bob Weir (far right), Jerry Garcia, and Mickey Hart performed with African musicians. As Blakesberg recalls, approximately 50,000 people attended the event.

Brent Mydland, 1952–1990 photograph by Jon Sievert/Getty Images

229

Shortly after the summer '90 tour, on July 26, Brent Mydland, age thirty-seven, overdosed on a speedball—a fatal shot of morphine and cocaine. Just twelve days earlier, at Massachusetts's Foxboro Stadium, during his last week of performances with the band, Mydland had sung "I Will Take You Home." "It was heartbreaking when Brent died," Jerry Garcia later said. "Here's this incredibly talented guy—he had a great natural melodic sense, and he was a great singer. And he could've gotten better, but he just didn't see it."

Vince Welnick and Bruce Hornsby, 1991 photograph by Susana Millman

230

Following Brent Mydland's death, the Dead asked keyboardist Bruce Hornsby
(right) to join the group. The Virginian's band the Range had already had a hit with
"The Way It Is," so he was reluctant to commit to a full-time gig with the Dead.
In August, former Tubes keyboardist Vince Welnick (left) auditioned, and thus the
band would frequently enjoy the services of two keyboardists, as during this gig
at the LA Coliseum on June 1, 1991.

Deadheads in Arizona, 1990 photograph by Susana Millman

233

Here, twenty-five years after the Grateful Dead's formation, a new generation of
Deadheads gathers at the Compton Terrace Amphitheatre, in Chandler, Arizona.
"There are people out there who look a whole lot like the people that we originally
started playing to," Jerry Garcia said in 1989. "So you get this kind of relativistic
view of time. We have people coming to our shows who are younger than we were
when we started."

Mike Brady and Bill Kreutzmann, 1990 by Susana Millman

234 At the Compton Terrace Amphitheatre on December 8, Ultra Sound's Mike Brady hangs with Bill Kreutzmann backstage before sound check. The UltraSound team, founded by John Meyer, provided extraordinary live sound for the band beginning in 1979.

Branford Marsalis with the Dead, 1990 photograph by Susana Millman

235

The band ended the year with its traditional New Year's Eve concert at the Oakland Coliseum Arena. The show was hosted by Word Jazz creator Ken Nordine—a hero of Jerry Garcia's—and opening act the Branford Marsalis Quartet. The great New Orleans–born musician also sat in with the Dead, as he had earlier in the year. Most Deadheads consider this one of the band's top New Year's Eve gigs. Seen here, Jerry Garcia, Bruce Hornsby, Branford Marsalis, Mickey Hart, and Vince Welnick (from left).

Robert Hunter and Jerry Garcia, 1991 photograph by Jay Blakesberg

236

"This was taken at the Dead office in San Rafael—my first portrait session with Garcia. I was brought in by *The Golden Road* to take pictures for an interview Blair Jackson was doing with Hunter and Garcia. This was a big deal because they'd never really done an interview together and almost never been photographed together. After the interview, Dennis McNally tells me I have five minutes—which is not exactly how I'd envisioned this, to say the least. For the first couple of minutes, they pretty much ignored me completely, talking to each other. And the whole time Dennis is tapping on the door, saying, 'You have one minute left!' So it wasn't exactly the best conditions, but some of the shots are my favorite Jerry portraits that I ever took. They're really sweet—he looks healthy. But it was all done in probably three minutes total."

—Jay Blakesberg

Mickey Hart and Joan Baez, 1991 photograph by Jay Blakesberg

237

During the first Gulf War, Mickey Hart performed at a Bring the Troops Home rally with Joan Baez, with whom he was briefly romantically involved. The gathering occurred at the San Francisco Civic Center Plaza.

Deadhead bus, 1991 photograph by Susana Millman

238

On April 28, 1991, en route to Las Vegas from Hoover Dam, Susana Millman spotted a Deadhead bus out the window. "This bus was a parking lot staple," Millman recalls, "and here it is streaking toward Las Vegas for the show. We were doing a little sightseeing and there it was! *We are everywhere!*" The day before, at the University of Nevada, in Las Vegas, the Grateful Dead's debut at the Sam Boyd Silver Bowl had initiated a new Deadhead tradition—annual pilgrimages to this gig.

Carlos Santana with the Grateful Dead, 1991 photograph by Susana Millman

239

Carlos Santana opened both shows at the Sam Boyd Silver Bowl in Las Vegas, and, as documented by Susana Millman, joined the band on "Bird Song," the first-set closer on April 28, 1991. Seen here, Bob Weir, Carlos Santana, Vince Welnick, and Jerry Garcia (from left). That same month, an album of Grateful Dead covers, *Deadicated*, was released, featuring contributions from Dwight Yoakam, Suzanne Vega, Dr. John, Los Lobos, Elvis Costello, and others.

Mickey Hart with a Gyuto monk, 1991 photograph by Susana Millman

240

In 1985, Mickey Hart first met and recorded the Gyuto Monks of Tibet, who could generate otherworldly vocal chants. He would continue to work with them over the years, and they would perform with the Dead on occasion. Susana Millman took this photo at Mickey Hart's home, where the monks were preparing for their second US tour, sponsored by Hart. "The presence of the monks made Mickey more the real person than the rock star," Millman recalls. "He did his own vacuuming to get ready for them!"

Jerry Garcia, Bruce Hornsby, and Vince Welnick, 1991 photograph by Susana Millman

241

During this August 1991 gig at Sacramento's Cal Expo Amphitheatre, Bruce Hornsby played accordion, which Jerry Garcia always loved. According to *Poughkeepsie Journal* music writer John Barry, who saw 200 Dead shows between 1987 and 1995, it was Garcia's exquisite guitar playing that turned the future journalist into a Deadhead. "The band never failed to go out there and take chances musically," says Barry, "even when it could mean failing miserably. That attitude inspired me to have the guts to try to make it as a music writer."

Bob Bralove, 1991 photograph by Susana Millman

242 Hanging near the Dead's sound control panels, Bob Bralove helped to provide the band's MIDI sound programming beginning in 1989. That same year, he also cowrote the song "Picasso Moon" with Bob Weir and John Perry Barlow. Here, Bralove takes care of business at the Cal Expo Amphitheatre.

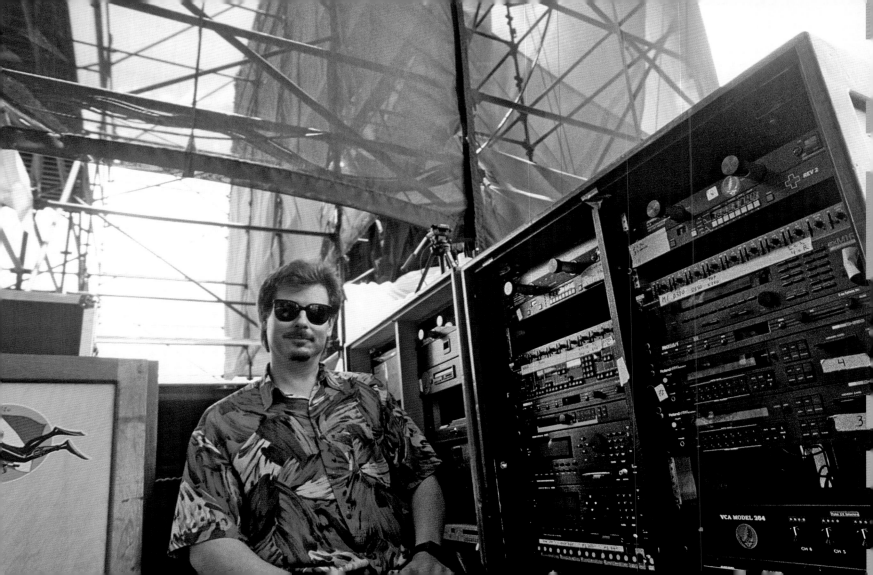

Jerry Garcia, 1991 photograph by Susana Millman

243

On August 24 and 25, 1991, Jerry Garcia played at the Gold Coast Concert Bowl, in Squaw Valley, California. The electric Jerry Garcia Band performed on the twenty-fourth; the acoustic show, including David Grisman, occurred on the twenty-fifth. "Windy conditions prevailed at the top of the ridge," Susana Millman remembers, "and the acoustic band was not happy with the tricks the wind played on the sound." That same month saw the release of a live album, *Jerry Garcia Band*, which features songs by Bob Dylan, Los Lobos, and Peter Tosh, among others.

Boston Garden, 1991 photograph by Susana Millman

244

"*We are everywhere* strikes again!" says Susana Millman of this September '91 billboard, on view outside the Boston Garden during the band's first gigs there in six years. "I had been thinking it would be fun to change the ad in Photoshop from NOTHING BEATS A BUD to NOTHING BEATS THE DEAD when I saw it the day before—and when we arrived the next day, the deed had been done for real!" Deadheads remember the six nights at the Garden as being some of the very best shows of the band's latter years.

Jerry Garcia, 1991 photograph by Jay Blakesberg

245

"[Jerry] is a virtuoso . . . the most generous musician I've ever met."

—Warren Zevon

Neil Young with the Grateful Dead, 1991 photograph by Jay Blakesberg

246 After the shocking and sudden death of Bill Graham on October 25, 1991, a memorial concert was held on Sunday, November 3, in San Francisco's Golden Gate Park. Neil Young joined the band for a version of his "Forever Young." Here, Phil Lesh, Bob Weir, Neil Young, and Jerry Garcia (from left).

Wavy Gravy and Ken Kesey, 1992 photograph by Susana Millman

249

At the Fat Tuesday concert on February 24, 1992 (actually held on a Monday), longtime Dead buddies Wavy Gravy (b. Hugh Romney) and Ken Kesey (right) help celebrate the three Oakland Coliseum Arena shows that marked the first concerts of the year for the Dead. Kesey frequently gave speeches at big Dead events, and once said of his first impression of the band, "They were a hairy, bad lookin' bunch of guys. I thought they were on their way to no good."

Noah's ark, 1992 photograph by Susana Millman

250

In a poignant reminder of their felled comrade Bill Graham, the Noah's ark float,
sponsored by the Bill Graham Presents organization, made an appearance at the
Dead's Mardi Gras concert.

Mardi Gras, 1992 photograph by Susana Millman

251

One of the Mardi Gras floats at the Dead concert featured a poster from a prior year when the Neville Brothers had opened, as well as a New Year's Eve poster. The February run featured four new songs—but did not include Bruce Hornsby, who had become increasingly disenchanted with Jerry Garcia's return to hard-drug use. The forthcoming spring tour would be Hornsby's last with the band.

Casey Jones train, 1992 photograph by Jay Blakesberg

252

"Trouble ahead." As the Casey Jones train plows forward on February 24, 1992, the band plays on—Phil Lesh, Bill Kreutzmann, Mickey Hart, Bob Weir, Jerry Garcia, and Vince Welnick (from left).

Bob Weir, 1992 photograph by Jay Blakesberg

253

In 1991, Bob Weir collaborated with his sister Wendy Weir on a children's book, *Panther Dream: A Story of the African Rainforest*. Jay Blakesberg took the authors' photos at Bob's home, where he also took this portrait. "I've shot Bob Weir at his house several times," says Blakesberg. "He has a beautiful, small A-frame house in Mill Valley, tucked away in the woods on the slopes of Mount Tamalpais. He's lived there since the early seventies. It's very quaint and rustic."

Jerry Garcia, 1992 photograph by Jay Blakesberg

254

Following the Dead's annual summer tour and a three-week outing with his solo band, Jerry Garcia suffered another collapse on August 3, 1992—two days after he turned fifty. He was diagnosed with respiratory ailments, an enlarged heart, and related health problems. The band canceled its fall shows, and Garcia concentrated on getting healthy. He dropped his junk—and junk food—habits. By December 10, when this photo was taken, he'd lost more than sixty pounds. During the year, Garcia's artwork had been exhibited at numerous galleries, and a book of his work had been published. Blakesberg took this portrait of a reinvigorated Garcia at the opening of his art exhibit at a Berkeley gallery.

The Dead return, 1992 photograph by Susana Millman

255

In early December, the Grateful Dead returned to performing, with a pair of shows at McNichols Sports Arena in Denver, followed by two outdoor concerts at the Compton Terrace Amphitheatre in Chandler, Arizona. On December 6, 1992, at Compton Terrace, Garcia—flanked by Bob Weir and Vince Welnick—appears a new man.

Jerry Garcia, 1992 photograph by Susana Millman

256

"[Jerry Garcia] could play just one note and the sound moved me so much. There was a very emotional, soulful quality to his tone. . . . It was very expressive. Great phrasing and articulation. It was nothing contrived. It was a very natural-sounding electric guitar."

—Bruce Hornsby

Harry Popick, 1992 photograph by Susana Millman

257

Harry Popick mans the Dead's monitor mixes. In 1992, when the group switched from using speaker monitors located onstage to using monitors worn in the ear, Popick continued to operate sound levels at the monitor console (seen here). According to Dead historian Dennis McNally, "Harry probably has the worst job in the Dead, because he is responsible for what the band will hear, and that is too painfully important." Here, Popick stands by at the Compton Terrace Amphitheatre on December 6.

Wavy Gravy and friend, 1992 photograph by Susana Millman

258 At the Oakland Coliseum Arena on December 11–13 and 16–17, the Dead played their last gigs of 1992—for the first time in years, they were taking off over the holidays to relax. Here, in the arena's backstage kids' room, pal Wavy Gravy has a little pre-holiday fun with young Salome Donenfeld. "This is a Photoshopped image," Susana Millman explains, "a visual pun since the wave filter is applied to Wavy Gravy's striped red and white shirt to create the background."

Deadorabilia, 1993 photograph by Jay Blakesberg

259

"The traveling caravan that followed the Grateful Dead in the late seventies was still quite small—just a few hundred people—and some of the friendships I forged then have lasted to this day. Traveling by car or bus or plane or by thumb only added to the adventure. Eventually, of course, I didn't want to miss a show—what if they played 'The Wheel' or 'Morning Dew' or, God forbid, 'Dark Star'? Alas, real-life issues kept me away from many shows, but I went when I could and I always had a blast."

—Jay Blakesberg

Carlos Santana and Jerry Garcia, 1993 photograph by Susana Millman

260

The Grateful Dead began 1993 performing at the Oakland Coliseum Arena—the same location at which they'd ended 1992. January 24–26 celebrated Chinese New Year, and February 21–23 marked Mardi Gras. Seen here on Tuesday, January 26, Carlos Santana joins the band on the second set, just after the drums segment (Mickey Hart can be seen in the back).

Chinese New Year, 1993 photograph by Susana Millman

261

The Grateful Dead loved the spectacle of the Chinese New Year parade. On January 26, 1993, while the drummers took over, a humongous dragon paraded through the crowd; at another point in the set, several oversize Chinese figures made an appearance on stilts.

Mardi Gras, 1993 photograph by Susana Millman

262 Every year at the Mardi Gras concerts, Deadheads tried to outdo themselves in their revelry and festive costumes—bringing a little bit of the French Quarter to the Oakland Coliseum Arena. On Fat Tuesday 1993, Phil Lesh gave fans another surprise—singing a new number for the Dead, a cover of Robbie Robertson's "Broken Arrow."

Ornette Coleman jams with the Dead, 1993 photograph by Susana Millman

263

Another highlight of the Mardi Gras show was Ornette Coleman's participation. He and his band Prime Time opened the show, and Jerry Garcia joined them during the end of their set. Coleman returned to the stage to play his famous white plastic saxophone with the Dead on "Drums" and, when this photo was taken, "The Other One." In 1988, Garcia had recorded with Coleman; Bob Weir recalled of the session, "Seeing Ornette live in the studio . . . that's when I realized this guy is doing things no one else has done. He's not playing the math, he's playing the emotion." Here, playing the emotion, Weir, Garcia, and Coleman (from left).

Pete Townshend and the Dead, 1993 photograph by Time Life Pictures/Getty Images

264

Since the sixties, the Grateful Dead had played with the Who several times, including at the Monterey Pop Festival in 1967, Woodstock in '69, the Oakland Coliseum Arena in '76, and again in 1981. The two bandleaders, Jerry Garcia and Pete Townshend, had particularly bonded during a later Dead/Who bill in England. Here, they pick up where they left off—Bill Kreutzmann, Bob Weir, Townshend, and Garcia (from left).

Signing baseballs, 1993 photograph by Susana Millman

265 For opening day of the baseball season in Candlestick Park, the San Francisco Giants invited members of the Dead to sing the National Anthem. Before the April 12 game got under way, Jerry Garcia and Bob Weir—wearing their Giants jackets— put their John Hancocks on a few balls.

Sam Boyd Silver Bowl, 1993 photograph by Jay Blakesberg

268   Capacity crowds filled the Las Vegas amphitheater for three days in May '93 to welcome back the Dead, with opening act Sting, who would go on to play a string of dates with the band. *Rolling Stone*'s Anthony DeCurtis wrote of the new coupling, "They make an unlikely pair . . . but Jerry Garcia and Sting seem to have hit it off quite nicely. . . . Garcia—whom Sting has genially dubbed Father Christmas—has taken to joining Sting onstage during his sets." Blakesberg captured their joint audience on May 15.

The Dead at the Silver Bowl, 1993 photograph by Jay Blakesberg

269

During their 1993 *Rolling Stone* interview, Jerry Garcia told Anthony DeCurtis, "Grateful Dead music is a holographic experience. It's made up of the points of view of all of the members of the band. Consequently, every angle that you look at it from, it's different. And a lot of times it's unpredictable. That's one of the things that makes it interesting to keep doing." From this angle, Phil Lesh, Bob Weir, Bill Kreutzmann, and Jerry Garcia (from left) on May 15.

Silver Bowl fans, 1993 photograph by Jay Blakesberg

270

"It used to be that you could run away and join the circus, say, or ride the freight trains. . . . [Following the Dead] is this time frame's version of the archetypal American adventure."

—Jerry Garcia

Deadheads, 1993 photograph by Jay Blakesberg

271

Grateful Dead fans twirl at the Shoreline Amphitheatre, in Mountain View, California, on May 21, 1993. "As a band, the Dead were inconsistent, at times pathetic," according to poet and writer Sparrow, who first saw the Grateful Dead in 1970. "But as a work of Shamanic divination, they were superb."

Phil Lesh, 1993 photograph by Jay Blakesberg

272

"To me, the Grateful Dead is life—the life of the spirit . . . [and] the mind, as opposed to standing in line and marking time in the twentieth century."

—Phil Lesh

Dan Healy, 1993 photograph by Susana Millman

275

California native Dan Healy began working for the Dead as soundman in 1966. He originally met the band during a Fillmore show at which Phil Lesh's amp broke; Healy, who was in the audience, fixed it. According to Healy, "I don't hassle destiny—there's some reason I'm here." He would spend nearly thirty years with the band, leaving in the spring of 1994. Here, he still enjoys the view.

Knobs, 1993 photograph by Susana Millman

276 So many knobs to turn! This section of Dan Healy's board affects the sound of Bill Kreutzmann's drum kit.

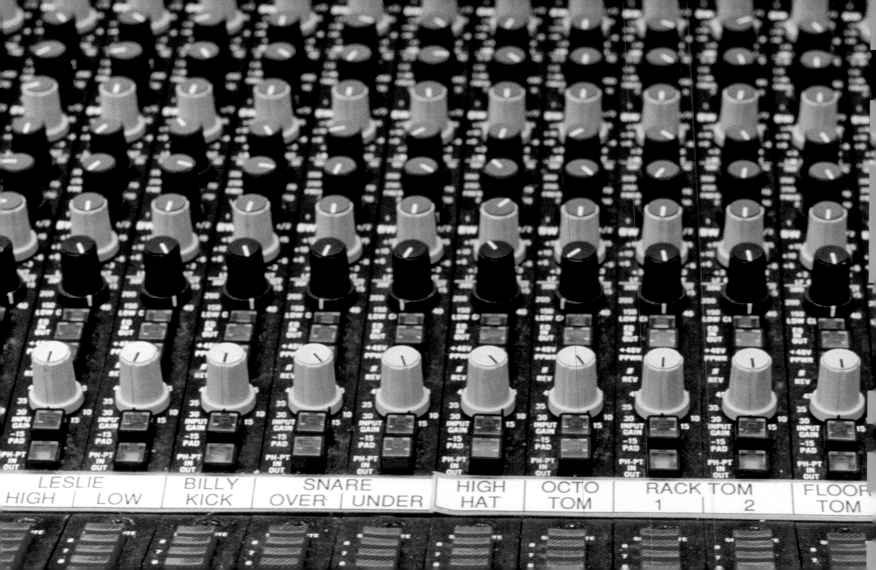

Bob Weir, Jerry Garcia, and Vince Welnick, Madison Square Garden, 1993 photograph by Ebet Roberts

277

"Going to Grateful Dead shows was the musical version of Major League Baseball," according to Deadhead Chris Cantergiani, who attended forty Dead concerts between 1989 and 1995. "If they were playing a series of three nights, you go all three because even though it's the same players and the same team, every night is different. You *might* be there for a very important and special night that has magic. Some nights your team loses. Some nights they hit countless home runs. Many people sitting in the stadium write in little notebooks details of that night's game. It's the same thing with the Grateful Dead."

Jerry Garcia and David Grisman, 1993 photograph by Jay Blakesberg

278

Jay Blakesberg photographed old pals Jerry Garcia and David Grisman at the latter's home in Mill Valley. Around this time, Garcia said of the mandolinist, his longtime buddy, "Grisman is a very rigorous musician. He likes to rehearse and get things down perfectly. He's a master of detail. I'm *not* those things, but we balance each other out." The two recorded a children's album of edgy folk songs, *Not for Kids Only*, released later that year.

Mardi Gras, 1994 photograph by Susana Millman

282 At their traditional Mardi Gras concert, on February 27 (a Sunday), 1994, the Dead welcomed an array of floats to the Oakland Coliseum Arena. *Skelvis*, designed by the Art Police, was a highlight.

Mickey Hart, 1994 photograph by Susana Millman

283

"People play music for different reasons. I go for the spirit side of things—not necessarily to be perfect."

—Mickey Hart

Phil Lesh, 1994 photograph by Susana Millman

284

"I've always called what we play 'electric chamber music.' . . . Chamber music has been called the music of friends."

—Phil Lesh

Bob Weir, 1994 photograph by Susana Millman

285

"We're a lot like the circus. . . . We won't give up until we feel we've achieved something."

—Bob Weir

Bill Kreutzmann, 1994 photograph by Susana Millman

286

"With the Grateful Dead, there's more possible than you could ever dream of—
even I could ever dream of. That's what's frustrating."

—Bill Kreutzmann

Dick Latvala, 1994 photograph by Susana Millman

287

The biggest Deadhead taper of all time, Dick Latvala followed the band since the Trips Festival. In 1985, he was named official Grateful Dead archivist by the band, and in December 1993 the debut in a series of *Dick's Picks* was released; this first vault recording documented a show in Tampa on December 19, 1973. Latvala, who died of a heart attack in 1999, once said, "Who in life can get the only possible job he could do? There's nothing else I know how to do. I can chew Doublemint and sit on a couch longer than anyone, but no one's going to pay money for that."

Bob Weir, Rob Wasserman, and Les Claypool, 1994 photograph by Jay Blakesberg

288

On March 2, 1994, at his Marin County home, Bob Weir posed for a portrait with bassist Rob Wasserman and Primus front man Les Claypool, both frequent collaborators. Wasserman's *Trios* album, featuring Weir and Claypool, had just been released. *BAM* magazine commissioned the photo for its cover.

Billy Grillo, 1994 photograph by Susana Millman

289

From March 4 to 6, 1994, the Grateful Dead performed at a venue new to them:
the Blockbuster Desert Sky Pavilion, in Phoenix, Arizona. On March 5, Susana
Millman took this photo of crew member Billy Grillo and his best friend, both
protecting their ears from the Dead's volume. "I thought I was going to get
thrown off the stage," Millman recalls, "but what Grillo wanted was for me
to take a picture of him with his dog!"

Harry Popick and Don Pearson, 1994 photograph by Susana Millman

290

At the March 5, 1994, Phoenix show, manning the monitor soundboards are longtime Grateful Dead crew Harry Popick (left) and Don Pearson.

Deadhead bus, 1994 photograph by Susana Millman

291

Parked in the lot at Las Vegas's Sam Boyd Silver Bowl, at the University of Nevada, is one of the many caravans that continued to follow the Dead. This group had driven from Montana. In some areas, though, Deadhead buses were cop magnets. "I bought a school bus, converted it to have a kitchen and sleeping for six—'Ramblin' Rose' was born," says Scott Elliot. "We were known for our really good spaghetti—three dollars, and if you wanted the 'special' sauce, it was five. She rode the interstates from 1987 to 1989, until the state of Tennessee didn't like the looks of a rainbow-painted school bus rollin' through their state."

Jerry Garcia and Grahame Lesh, 1994 photograph by Susana Millman

294

Phil Lesh's son Grahame enjoys his own private Jerry Garcia guitar solo at the Shoreline Amphitheatre, where the Grateful Dead came back for three more nights in September.

Cityscape floats, 1995 photograph by Jay Blakesberg

297

These Mardi Gras floats pay tribute to artist Rick Griffin with the artwork he created for the band's twentieth anniversary a decade earlier. Upon Griffin's death in 1991, Garcia said, "Oh, God, what a most painful experience. . . . He was one of those guys that you only get to see two or three times a year, but every time you do see him, you really enjoy it. That's the kind of relationship I had with Rick Griffin. I really respect him as an artist. I've been a fan of his since the sixties. And he was a real sweet person. Now I'm not gonna be able to look into those blue eyes."

Rhythm Devils, 1995 photograph by Susana Millman

298 Known by fans as the Rhythm Devils, Mickey Hart (center) and Bill Kreutzmann enjoy getting into the groove with other drummers. Here, on February 26, 1995, they jam with Sikiru Adepoju while the floats parade through the Oakland Coliseum Arena.

Two Jerrys, 1995 photograph by Susana Millman

299

On April 16, 1995, just prior to a US tour of the Gyuto Monks of Tibet, Mickey
Hart invited his bandmates and friends to a gathering at his Sonoma County
home. Here, Jerry Garcia and former California governor Jerry Brown engage
with two monks.

Gyuto Monks gathering, 1995 photograph by Susana Millman

300

"The monks performed a ceremony where they presented the guests with a white silk scarf from their order," explains photographer Susana Millman. Here, watching the monks (at left), are Dave Dennison, Caryl Ohrbach Hart, Mickey Hart, Reverend Matthew Fox, Anne Gust, Deborah Koons Garcia, Jerry Brown (partially obscured), and Jerry Garcia, who seems more interested in the camera than in the monks.

Mr. and Mrs. Jerry Garcia, 1995 photograph by Susana Millman

301

On Valentine's Day 1994, Jerry Garcia had wed for the third time, with Reverend Matthew Fox (at left) officiating at Christ Episcopal Church in Sausalito. Independent filmmaker Deborah Koons (center) and Garcia had been romantically entangled in the 1970s during Garcia's on-again-off-again relationship with Mountain Girl (who he eventually married and divorced). After Garcia and Koons bumped into each other in a health food store during the spring of 1993, their romance rekindled. Here, the newlyweds kid around with the priest who married them.

Ashley Judd and Jerry Garcia, 1995 photograph by Jay Blakesberg

302

The Jerry Garcia Band recorded two songs for the soundtrack to the Wayne Wang film *Smoke*, which also features a Garcia cameo. (The filmmaker had once worked as a roadie for the Dead.) The last-ever recordings by the Jerry Garcia Band, the tracks included Jerome Kern's "Smoke Gets in Your Eyes"—the only time Garcia cut a song by the composer for whom he was named. Here, Garcia and *Smoke*'s star Ashley Judd, with Garcia Band vocalists—or Jerryettes—Gloria Jones and Jackie LaBranch behind them.

Girl with bubbles, 1995 photograph by Susana Millman

310

A fan amuses herself at Giants Stadium. "It was amazing for me to be able to grow up with the Grateful Dead," remarks DJ Rick Schneider, who saw 150 Dead shows between 1980 and 1995. "Their music took me to places I never would have gone. The way they blended jazz, bluegrass, folk, rock, and psychedelia opened me up to all kinds of sounds, eventually leading me to radio, to becoming a DJ."

Jerry Garcia, 1942–1995 photograph by Susana Millman

313

Following the summer tour, Jerry Garcia entered the recording studio one last time; he cut a Jimmie Rodgers song, "Blue Yodel #9," for Bob Dylan's Rodgers tribute album. Soon after, he checked into the Betty Ford Center to kick his heroin addiction; two weeks later, he left and spent his fifty-third birthday at home. Then on August 8, he entered Serenity Knolls, a rehab center in Marin County. There, early the next morning, he died in his sleep of a massive heart attack. Five days before his death, he had called his old friend Robert Hunter and talked about the work they'd done together: "I've been singing some of those songs for over twenty-five years and they never once stuck in my throat," he told Hunter. "I always felt like they were saying what I wanted to be sayin'."

Jerry Garcia memorial, 1995 photograph by Evan Agostini/Getty Images

314

A private funeral was held for Jerry Garcia at St. Stephen's Episcopal Church on August 11, 1995. The Jerryettes and David Grisman performed and placed a guitar pick in Garcia's casket. Robert Hunter gave the eulogy: "Now that the singer has gone / Where shall I go for the song? / . . . May she bear thee to thy rest / Beyond the solitude of days / The tyranny of hours / The wreath of shining laurel lie / Upon your shaggy head / Bestowing power to play the lyre / To legions of the dead."

Wavy Gravy says good-bye, 1995 photograph by Kim Komenich/Getty Images

315

On August 13, 1995, a memorial tribute to Jerry Garcia took place in San Francisco's Golden Gate Park, at the Polo Field, where nearly three decades before the first Human Be-In had occurred. Here, the usually antic Wavy Gravy has a quiet moment.

Golden Gate Park, 1995 photograph by Susana Millman

316 Floral tributes to Jerry Garcia abounded at his public memorial to which an estimated 25,000 fans flocked. "There was a giant altar set up on risers," photographer Susana Millman recalls, "and it was filled and filled with flowers, photos, and many small tokens of great love."

Remembrance fence, 1995 photograph by Susana Millman

317

"There is no way to measure his greatness as a person or a player. . . . He really had no equal. To me he wasn't only a musician and friend, he was more like a big brother who taught and showed me more than he'll ever know."

—Bob Dylan

Farewell, 1995 photograph by Susana Millman

318

Bob Weir (center) was performing in New Hampshire with his band RatDog on the day Jerry Garcia died. "If our dear, departed friend proved anything to us," he told the grieving audience, "he proved that great music will remain." The great Babatunde Olatunji (in white dashiki) led a rhythmic and vocal invocation at the memorial, then introduced Deborah Koons Garcia (to his left) to address the crowd.

Golden Gate Park assemblage, 1995 photograph by Susana Millman

319

"If the Grateful Dead did anything, we gave you the power. . . . You have the groove, you have the feeling. We've been working on it for thirty years now. So what are you going to do with it? That's the question."

—Mickey Hart

Drum recessional, 1995 photograph by Jay Blakesberg

320

For the gathering at Golden Gate Park, Dick Latvala and David Gans chose a mix of Dead songs, which were played through massive speakers. During the drum recessional, "Not Fade Away" gave the perfect soundtrack to the march. Here, Phil Lesh is accompanied by his son Grahame and his wife, Jill, holding their youngest son, Brian.

Garcia shrine, 1995 photograph by Jay Blakesberg

321

All over San Francisco, makeshift tributes to Jerry Garcia were set up, many including photos taken by Jay Blakesberg. "The beauty of the Grateful Dead was their relationship with their fans," Wavy Gravy once said. "They just take this great big ball of love and bounce it out to the fans and the fans bounce it back, and each time it just gets bigger."

Central Park gathering, 1995 photograph by Evan Agostini/Getty Images

322

Impromptu gatherings were held in cities around the country to mourn the passing of Jerry Garcia. Here, fans gather in New York City's Central Park.

Ken Kesey and Wavy Gravy, 1995 photograph by Susana Millman

323

At a gathering at Wavy Gravy's Camp Winnarainbow in northern California, mourning for Jerry Garcia's death continued. As a foreword to a *Rolling Stone* tribute book to Garcia, Kesey wrote a letter to his pal: "I caught your funeral. . . . What really stood out—stands out—is the thundering silence, the lack, the absence of that golden Garcia lead line, of that familiar slick lick with the uptwist at the end, that merry snake twining through the woodpile, flickering in and out of the loosely stacked chords . . . a wriggling mystery, bright and slick as fire . . . suddenly gone."

The survivors, 1996 photograph by John Storey/Getty Images

324 In December 1995 the remaining members of the band met to determine their future. Bill Kreutzmann announced he no longer wished to tour, and they all agreed to retire the name Grateful Dead. During the summer of 1996, various members' bands took part in what became known as the Further tour. Here, on June 13, Mickey Hart, Bob Weir, Phil Lesh, and Vince Welnick (from left).

Further tour, 1996 photograph by Susana Millman

325 At the Virginia Beach stop of the Further tour, old friends gather for some laughs: Paul Magid (aka Dmitri of the Flying Karamazov Brothers), Bruce Hornsby, Bob Weir, Mickey Hart, and Hart's daughter Reya.

Bob Weir, 1996 photograph by Jay Blakesberg

326

On November 14, 1996, Bob Weir stopped by San Francisco's ArtRock Gallery
for the exhibition called the Art of the Dead. The rare poster next to Weir is
Trip or Freak.

Inaugural ball, 1997 photograph by Susana Millman

327

President Bill Clinton and, particularly, Vice President Al Gore were longtime Dead fans. The band visited Gore at the White House during the first Clinton/Gore term. On January 20, 1997, RatDog was one of the performers at the Tennessee Inaugural Ball, in Washington, DC. Seen here are Rob Wasserman, Bob Weir, President Clinton, Matthew Kelly, and Hillary Clinton (from left).

Al Gore speaks, 1997 photograph by Susana Millman

328

At the Tennessee Inaugural Ball, on January 20, 1997, Bob Weir, Tipper Gore, and Rickie Lee Jones (from left) lend an ear to Vice President Al Gore.

Further Festival, 1997 photograph by Susana Millman

329

For the second summer, the Further tour included former members of the Grateful Dead. Here, at an August 2 stop at the Shoreline Amphitheatre, RatDog is joined by Robert Hunter (second from left) and Black Crowes vocalist Chris Robinson (far right). The circuit marked Hunter's first public performances in seven years. Mickey Hart's band Planet Drum, moe., Jorma Kaukonen, and the Black Crowes were among the others on the tour.

Bob Weir and Bonnie Raitt, 1997 photograph by Susana Millman

330

Another guest at the August 2, 1997, RatDog performance was Bonnie Raitt, who played her bluesy guitar. Phil Lesh (far left) also stopped by during the act and jammed with Raitt, Bob Weir, Mickey Hart, and Bruce Hornsby.

Mickey Hart and friends, 1998 photograph by Jay Blakesberg

331

"I went to Mickey's spread in Sonoma County to shoot him for the cover of *Modern Drummer* magazine. He has a giant recording studio in a separate building down from his house, right next to a pond, so my assistant and I went in there and spent an hour moving his drums and percussion instruments together for the shot I wanted. The centerpiece was going to be a giant gong that Mickey was going to sit in front of, surrounded by instruments. We had probably moved twenty or thirty drums when Mickey shows up and says, 'What are you doing? You've gotta get this one and that one,' and he points at all these other drums. In true Mickey Hart fashion, he got everyone who was there standing around to get into the act. We spent more time moving drums into position than we did doing the shoot, because Mickey, notoriously, was in a hurry. You get ten minutes with him and you're done."

—Jay Blakesberg

Phil Lesh with bass, 1999 photograph by Jay Blakesberg

332

Jay Blakesberg shot this evocative image of Phil Lesh with his bass at the Warfield Theatre on April 16, 1999. The second in a trio of performances, this was the first outing for Phil Lesh and Friends since Lesh's lifesaving liver transplant the previous December, necessitated by a debilitating case of hepatitis C. Guests included former Dead vocalist Donna Jean Godchaux MacKay (who had remarried) and Phish members Trey Anastasio and Page McConnell.

Tom Constanten and Vince Welnick, 1999 photograph by Brian Hineline/Retna

333 On August 7, 1999, two former Grateful Dead keyboardists, Tom Constanten and Vince Welnick, perform in partnership at the Gathering on the Mountain, in Blakeslee, Pennsylvania.

Trey Anastasio and Phil Lesh, 1999 photograph by Jay Blakesberg

334

Phil Lesh joined Phish onstage at their Shoreline Amphitheatre gig on September 17, 1999. Inspired by the Grateful Dead, bands like Phish and moe. had started a whole new jam-band movement that attracted traveling fans, latter-day Deadheads of sorts. Jay Blakesberg photographed Trey Anastasio and Phil Lesh before the gig for *Guitar World* magazine.

Bob Weir's wedding day, 1999 photograph by Susana Millman

335

On July 15, longtime bachelor (and Dead heartthrob) Bob Weir tied the knot with Natascha Muenter. Toasting the happy couple (at far left) are Phil and Jill Lesh and Mickey and Caryl Ohrbach Hart (from left).

Phil Lesh and Friends onstage, 2001 photograph by Daniel Coston

336

Phil Lesh and Friends comprised a variety of players over the years. Guitarist Jimmy Herring (second from left), who had played with Atlanta's Col. Bruce Hampton and the Aquarium Rescue Unit, became a regular member in 2000 and would go on to perform with the Other Ones and the Dead. North Carolina–born Warren Haynes (far right) played with Lesh when not on the road with his Gov't Mule or the Allman Brothers Band. Keyboardist Rob Barraco (far left) had been a member of the Zen Tricksters, a group that played jazz-tinged improvisations of Grateful Dead songs.

Phil Lesh and Friends, 2002 photograph by Jay Blakesberg

337

Known for their superb musicianship, Phil Lesh and Friends became a popular concert draw. Jay Blakesberg took this publicity portrait of the group: Warren Haynes, Jimmy Herring, Lesh, keyboardist Rob Barraco, and Lesh's consistent drummer, John Molo (from left).

The Other Ones, 2002 photograph by Jay Blakesberg

338

During the summer of 2002, the "core four"—Bill Kreutzmann, Mickey Hart, Bob Weir, and Phil Lesh—reunited, and, with members of RatDog and Phil Lesh and Friends, put together the Other Ones. (Previously the Other Ones performed during the '98 Further Festival, minus Lesh and Kreutzmann.) This lineup toured in the fall of 2002—Weir, Kreutzmann, RatDog guitarist Jeff Chimenti, Jimmy Herring, Hart, Lesh, and Rob Barraco (from left). "The tour was a gas!" Lesh later said.

Bob Weir, 2002 photograph by Daniel Coston

339

Here, Bob Weir appears onstage in Charlotte, North Carolina, with RatDog, the band with whom he continues to tour. "When RatDog began playing the incredibly complex 'Terrapin Suite,' I thought it was really great to see Bob Weir take on that challenge," says music journalist John Barry. "It showed me that Jerry might be gone, but that the spirit of adventure that drove the Grateful Dead lives on."

Announcing the Dead, 2003 photograph by Susana Millman

340

On February 14, 2003, after the success of the Other Ones' tour the previous fall, the "core four" plus others performed as the Dead for the first time. The gig, at San Francisco's Warfield Theatre, benefited the Rex Foundation. Earlier in the month, the band announced, "After we played our first shows together at Alpine Valley last year, we were all profoundly affected by a sense of awe and connection that none of us had felt since we played with Jerry. . . . We had stopped being the Other Ones and were on our way to becoming something new but at the same time very familiar. . . .With the greatest possible respect to our collective history, we have decided to keep the name Grateful Dead retired in honor of Jerry's memory, and call ourselves: The Dead."

First night of the Dead, 2003 photograph by Susana Millman

341

Onstage at the Warfield Theatre, Rhythm Devils Bill Kreutzmann and Mickey Hart, and guitarist/vocalist Bob Weir. Debuting that night with the band was vocalist Joan Osborne.

Sammy Hagar with the Dead, 2003 photograph by Jay Blakesberg

342 Stopping by to sing with his old pals at the Warfield was Sammy Hagar (center), here flanked by Phil Lesh and Bob Weir, with Kreutzmann visible behind the drum kit. Robert Hunter opened the show.

The Dead, 2003 photograph by Jay Blakesberg

343

The Dead began rehearsing at the Warehouse, in Novato, California, in preparation for their first tour. Blakesberg took the publicity pictures for the band. (Front row) Jeff Chimenti, Joan Osborne, Bob Weir, Bill Kreutzmann (from left); (back row) Rob Barraco, Jimmy Herring, Mickey Hart, and Phil Lesh (from left).

Rhythm Devils, 2003 photograph by Jay Blakesberg

346 Following a Bonnaroo appearance, the Dead kick off their summer tour at Virginia Beach, with Bill Kreutzmann and Mickey Hart pounding out their traditional jam.

The Dead, 2003 photograph by Jay Blakesberg

347

The road warriors are ready for the summer tour: Phil Lesh, Bill Kreutzmann, Jeff Chimenti, Bob Weir, Rob Barraco, Mickey Hart, Jimmy Herring, and Joan Osborne (from left).

Phil Lesh and Bill Kreutzmann, 2003 photograph by Jay Blakesberg

348 On July 7, 2003, the Dead played one of the most spectacular venues in America, Colorado's Red Rocks; Lesh looks particularly pleased. The band would play five nights there.

The Dead at Red Rocks, 2003 photograph by Jay Blakesberg

349

On July 8, 2003, playing another night at Red Rocks are Phil Lesh, Bill Kreutzmann, Joan Osborne, Mickey Hart, and Bob Weir (from left). Kentucky native Osborne had been a regular on the New York City club circuit before scoring a huge hit in 1995 with "One of Us." According to *The Illustrated Dead*, "With her devotion to roots music and warm yet powerful voice, Osborne gave the Dead a vocal range and strength unmatched since the Donna Godchaux era." Osborne would also perform with Phil Lesh and Friends.

Making tracks, 2003 photograph by Jay Blakesberg

350

Here, in another Blakesberg publicity shot from Novato, are (front row) Jeff Chimenti, Joan Osborne, and Rob Barraco (from left); (back row) Mickey Hart, Bob Weir, Bill Kreutzmann, Phil Lesh, and Jimmy Herring (from left).

Dylan and the Dead, 2003 photograph by Jay Blakesberg

351

On August 3, 2003, the Dead performed with Garcia's old pal Bob Dylan. Seen here, Bob Weir, Dylan, and Jimmy Herring (from left). Dylan and his band would also tour with Phil Lesh and Friends.

Back-to-back, 2003 photograph by Jay Blakesberg

352 Mickey Hart and Bill Kreutzmann, here at the Dead's August 3, 2003, performance,
make an incredible rhythm team.

The Dead, 2003 photograph by Jay Blakesberg

353

Near the end of the third leg of their Summer Getaway tour are Jimmy Herring, Bob Weir, and Phil Lesh (from left).

Red Rocks, 2004 photograph by Jay Blakesberg

354

The Dead returned to Red Rocks for additional performances the following summer, as seen here on June 14, 2004.

RatDog on VH1, 2005 photograph by Billy Tompkins/Retna

355

Here, on May 4, 2005, RatDog jams at VH1 studios in New York City: Jeff Chimenti, Kenny Brooks, Jay Lane, Bob Weir, and Robin Sylvester (from left). The band has been releasing a series of live recordings since 2003.

Phil Lesh, 2005 photograph by Daniel Coston

356

On a double bill with RatDog in 2005, Phil Lesh and Friends leave their mark on Charlotte, North Carolina. Band members of the two groups often join each other onstage.

Bob Weir, 2005 photograph by Daniel Coston

357 Bob Weir plays with RatDog on a double bill with Phil Lesh and Friends in Charlotte, North Carolina.

Comes a Time tribute to Jerry Garcia, 2005 photograph by Susana Millman

358 On September 24, 2005, to mark the tenth anniversary of Jerry Garcia's death, his friends, family, and bandmates gathered at the Greek Theatre, in Berkeley, for a tribute concert. Proceeds went to the Rex Foundation. Seen here, Jackie LaBranch, Bruce Hornsby, Donna Jean Godchaux MacKay, Bob Weir, and Gloria Jones (from left).

Jerry's daughters, 2005 photograph by Susana Millman

359 At the Comes a Time tribute, three of Jerry Garcia's daughters, Annabelle Garcia, Heather Katz, and Teresa "Trixie" Garcia (from left) are captured by Susana Millman's lens. Annabelle and Trixie are the daughters of Mountain Girl and Jerry; a concert violinist, Heather is Jerry's eldest daughter with his first wife, Sarah Katz.

Phil Lesh and friends, 2005 photograph by Jay Blakesberg

360

Blakesberg snapped this portrait of Phil Lesh with his exquisite collection of instruments for *Bass Player* magazine. "Phil plays genius music," says one longtime follower of the Grateful Dead.

Mickey Hart, 2006 photograph by Andrew Marks/Retna

361

On April 21, 2006, Mickey Hart showed his green side in an appearance at an Earth Day celebration in New York City. With him is Mike Gordon, former member of Phish.

Vince Welnick, 1952–2006 photograph by Daniel Coston

362

Fulfilling the curse of the Grateful Dead keyboardists, Vince Welnick passed away on June 2, 2006. He had suffered from severe depression following Jerry Garcia's death but had eventually pulled out of it and formed a band called the Missing Man Formation. He continued to perform up until his death at age fifty-four.

Bob Weir and Donna Jean Godchaux MacKay, 2007 photograph by Susana Millman

363

On September 20, 2007, the Mill Valley hangout Sweetwater opened its doors for the last time. To pay tribute to a favorite neighborhood place, Bob Weir performed, with Donna Jean Godchaux MacKay helping out on vocals. MacKay continues to perform around the country, with her group Donna Jean and the Tricksters, which released an album in 2008.

Phil Lesh and Friends, 2008 photograph by Jay Blakesberg

364

John Molo, Jackie Greene, Steve Molitz, Larry Campbell, and Phil Lesh: The latest incarnation of Phil Lesh and Friends keeps a busy schedule, selling out multinight runs in New York City and performing at festivals nationally.

Dead reunion, 2008 photograph by Jay Blakesberg

365

In February 2008, on the eve of Super Tuesday, the Dead reunited to play a benefit for Barack Obama at San Francisco's Warfield Theatre. Prior to showtime, Jay Blakesberg, who directed a live concert Webcast of the event, photographed Bob Weir, Mickey Hart, and Phil Lesh. "Eighty-five thousand people watched the concert on iClips.net," says Blakesberg. "It was a special night—everyone was very pleased with the music and the vibe. All of these Dead members have strong projects going on their own, but they are still—and always will be—brothers."

"WHAT A LONG STRANGE TRIP ITS BEEN

First of all, if not for the Grateful Dead. . . . *Muchas gracias* for the music and the scene it created. Many thanks to those astute Grateful Dead scholars whose work provided so much insight and information as I researched the band, especially Dennis McNally, Blair Jackson, and the team responsible for *Grateful Dead: The Illustrated Trip*, as well as those behind the superb Web site www.dead.net. I'm also very grateful to Rick Schneider, Steve Gorman, Gregg Goldman, Peter McQuaid, Bernadette Cummings, Chris Cantergiani, Steve Glasenk, John Barry, Ruth Ellen Gruber, Anmarie Linsley, James Austin, Karla Buhlman, Maddy Miller, Barbara Redfield, Sparrow, Graham Parker, Rob and Ursula at the Wine Hutch, and Damien Toman for their help. Of course, without the cooperation and fantastic work of the photographers, as well as Retna's Jon Espinosa, Jens Jurgensen at Ebet Roberts Studio, Dianne Duenzl at Baron Wolman's Studio, and Jonathan Hyams, Dina Greenberg, and Helen Ashford at Getty Images, this book would not exist. Jay Blakesberg spent hours on the phone with me, and Susana Millman, Amalie R. Rothschild, Stanley Mouse, Ebet Roberts, Baron Wolman, Jim Marshall, Bob Leafe, and Stephanie Chernikowski were very generous with their time. Thanks to the folks at Abrams—Deborah Aaronson, Sarah Gifford, Laura Tam, Alison Gervais, Steve Tager, and Michael Jacobs—for their expertise and enthusiasm. I'd also like to thank Carrie Hornbeck and Nina Pearlman for their editorial precision. As always, Robert and Jack Warren offered their love and support. Finally, thanks to my old buddies at Chapel Hill's 608 Airport Road, who accompanied me on that extraordinary "trip" to my first-ever Dead concert at Duke University's Cameron Indoor Stadium on September 23, 1976. I can't say I remember much— but I think that means I was there.

Acknowledgments

Sources

Many of the quotes and much of the research came from the following sources:

Between the Dark and Light: The Grateful Dead Photography of Jay Blakesberg, by Jay Blakesberg and the Grateful Dead, Backbeat Books, 2004

Bill Graham Presents: My Life Inside Rock and Out, by Bill Grapham and Robert Greenfield, Doubleday, 1992

Book of the Dead: Celebrating 25 Years with the Grateful Dead, by Herb Greene, Delacorte Press, 1990

Freehand: The Art of Stanley Mouse, by Stanley Mouse et al., Snow Lion Graphics/SLG Books, 1992

Garcia, by the editors of *Rolling Stone*, Little, Brown and Company, 1995

Garcia: An American Life, by Blair Jackson, Viking Adult, 1999

Grateful Dead: The Golden Road (1965–1973) box set, liner notes by James Austin, David Lemieux, Connie Bonner Mosley, Dennis McNally, and Ihor Slabicky, Rhino, 2001

Grateful Dead: The Illustrated Trip, foreword by Robert Hunter, produced in collaboration with Grateful Dead Productions, with contributions from Blair Jackson, Dennis McNally, Stephen Peters, and Chuck Wills, DK, 2003

Live at the Fillmore East: A Photographic Memoir, by Amalie R. Rothschild with Ruth Ellen Gruber, Thunder's Mouth Press, 1999

Living with the Dead: Twenty Years on the Bus with Garcia and the Grateful Dead, by Rock Scully and David Dalton, Little, Brown and Company, 1995

A Long Strange Trip: The Inside History of the Grateful Dead, by Dennis McNally, Broadway, 2002

Rhino has done an amazing job reissuing the Dead's albums and releasing live recordings and other material over the years. These should not be missed—even by those who, like me, still have their Grateful Dead vinyl. The Sirius Satellite Radio channel devoted to the Grateful Dead and, of course, www.dead.net are additional excellent sources for Dead music and information. Also, in 2008, Shout Factory reissued Mickey Hart's recordings—they are highly recommended for fans of world music and percussion.

Credits

and we bid you
good night
good night
good night

Index

Page numbers in *italics* refer to illustrations.

Project Manager: Deborah Aaronson
Editor: Laura Tam
Designer: Sarah Gifford
Production Manager: Alison Gervais

Library of Congress Cataloging-in-Publication Data

George-Warren, Holly.
  Grateful Dead 365 / by Holly George-Warren.
    p. cm.
  ISBN 978-0-8109-7282-7
  1. Grateful Dead (Musical group) 2. Rock musicians—United
States—Biography. I. Title.

  ML421.G72G46 2008
  782.42166092'2—dc22
                    2008017512

Printed and bound in China
10 9 8 7 6 5 4 3 2 1

Abrams books are available at special discounts when purchased in quantity for premiums and promotions
as well as fundraising or educational use. Special editions can also be created to specification. For details,
contact specialmarkets@hnabooks.com or the address below.

HNA ■■■■■
harry n. abrams, inc.
a subsidiary of La Martinière Groupe
115 West 18th Street
New York, NY 10011
www.hnabooks.com

Dedicated to Grateful Dead fans everywhere

FRONT COVER
San Francisco, 1966. Photograph
by Jim Marshall.

BACK COVER
Sky River Festival, Washington, 1968.
Photograph by Jim Marshall.

ENDPAPERS
New Year's balloon drop,
Henry J. Kaiser Convention Center,
Oakland, California, 1986.
Photograph by Susana Millman.